DAILY OU

THE
PENNINE WAY

WALKS FOR YOUNG AND OLD

by

HARRY PENRICE

Cartoons and front cover by Phil Turner

Thornhill Press

Published by
Thornhill Press
24 Moorend Road
Cheltenham, Glos

MCMXCI

ISBN 0 946328 32 3

**PLEASE RESPECT THE ENVIRONMENT
AND KEEP TO THE COUNTRY CODE**

Typeset in Times by
Cotswold Typesetting Limited, Cheltenham
Printed by
Billing & Sons Ltd, Worcester

THE
PENNINE WAY

The numbers indicate the
approximate location of
40 walks, some circular,
some out and home, which
incorporate the entire
Pennine Way.

Each walk is described
in the ensuing pages.
Actual directions are in
italics, whilst descriptive
matter is in standard type,
and basic route maps show
the actual walk locations.

Map references relate to
OS maps 1:50,000.

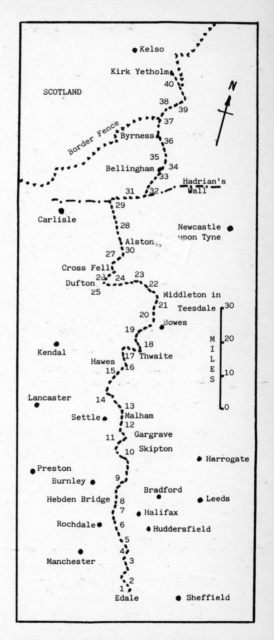

iii

WALKS ALONG THE PENNINE WAY

Walk	Section	Miles	Page
1	Edale to Kinder Downfall	9	5
2	Kinder Downfall to Snake Pass	10	9
3	Snake Pass to Crowden	14	13
4	Saddleworth Road (A635) to Crowden	13	17
5	Saddleworth Road (A635) to Buckstones (A640)	12	21
6	Buckstones (A640) to Blackstone Edge (A58)	11	23
7	Blackstone Edge (A58) to Stoodley Pike	11	27
8	Stoodley Pike to Colden	11	31
9	Colden to Cowling	15	37
10	Cowling to Thornton-in-Craven	14	41
11	Thornton-in-Craven to Gargrave	14	45
12	Gargrave to Malham Tarn	13	47
13	Malham Tarn to Silverdale Road	13	51
14	Silverdale Road to Horton-in-Ribblesdale	12	55
15	Horton-in-Ribblesdale to Cam Houses	16	59
16	Cam Houses to Gayle	14	63
17	Gayle to Thwaite	11	65
18	Thwaite to Stonehouse Moor	11	69
19	Stonehouse Moor to Sleightholme	13	73
20	Sleightholme to Clove Lodge, Baldersdale	14	77
21	Clove Lodge, Baldersdale to Middleton-in-Teesdale	13	81
22	Middleton-in-Teesdale to Saur Hill Bridge	16	85
23	Saur Hill Bridge to Cauldron Snout	11	89
24	Cauldron Snout to High Cup Nick	14	93
25	High Cup Nick to Dufton	11	97
26	Dufton to Teeshead	16	101
27	Teeshead to Garrigill	16	105
28	Alston to Lambley (A689)	12	109
29	Lambley to Great Chesters	15	113
30	Garrigill to Harbutt Lodge, Alston	6	117
31	Great Chesters to Hotbank Crags	14	121
32	Hotbank Crags to Warks Burn	18	123

Walk	Section	Miles	Page
33	Bellingham to Hareshaw Head (B6320)	8	127
34	Warks Burn to Bellingham	16	131
35	Hareshaw Head (B6320) to Redesdale Forest Gate	15	133
36	Redesdale Forest Gate to Byrness YHA	13	137
37	Byrness YHA to Chew Green	15	139
38	Chew Green to Kirk Yetholm	12	145
39	Lamb Hill to Windy Gyle	11	149
40	Windy Gyle to Kirk Yetholm	21	153

ACKNOWLEDGEMENTS

I would like to thank the family for the support and transport they so readily supplied to make this adventure less arduous. My special thanks go to my daughter-in-law, Barbara, whose nimble fingers changed my amateurish typing into a beautifully prepared manuscript, and to Alan Goldsbro, whose equipment and word processing wizardry relieved me of this frightening task.

My most special thanks, appreciation and admiration go to my wife, Nancy, for her companionship on every inch of the Pennine Way, over hills and dales, and through peat bogs and water; and she unfailingly augmented this effort with a well-prepared menu. Her support and encouragement in preparing this book has been invaluable, and her position as proof reader absolutely essential.

DAILY OUTINGS ON THE PENNINE WAY

INTRODUCTION

Windy Gyle, Cauldron Snout, Hadrian's Wall, Kinder Scout. These names create visions of austere beauty, ancient history and frightening loneliness, and they have all one connecting thread— the Pennine Way.

We had been to them all and nurtured pipe dreams of walking that notorious footpath, but there was one major problem, my wife and I were both past that dreaded sixty fifth birthday. Reading Tom Stephenson's "Pennine Way" and Wainwright's "Companion" increased the desire but did nothing to solve the problem. We pondered over the various approaches. Backpacking with massive rucksacks, and sleeping rough, was something for younger people. Youth hostelling, with only seven or eight within reasonable distance of the path, in 270 miles, was out. Bed and breakfasting was equally difficult, and too expensive for the average old age pensioner to contemplate.

It was an unknown walker on the summit of Close Hill, near Edale, who provided the solution. He had walked the Pennine Way at weekends, with a friend providing transport to the start and from the finish of each walk, with a stay at a nearby pub on the Saturday night. Working on the idea of a series of short walks, maps were studied to see how we could apply this technique using our caravan, and doing our own driving. Circular or out and home walks would be essential, and our progress would be halved, but we had plenty of time and were not restricted to weekends.

The winter months were spent planning daily walks from suitable access points. We found there were about thirty crossing points on classified roads, and several on minor roads, so all we had to do was find a campsite which was fairly close to a suitable crossing. A few miles' drive from the site to the start of the walk was no problem. Our target was a walk of not more than ten to twelve miles in a day, and we roughed out about fifty walks. We decided that we were not going to restrict ourselves to making the walks in any pre-ordained order, and we didn't care which way we walked the Pennine Way, so long as we covered every foot of it.

We talked it over with the family, and got some offers of help with

1

transport, and we checked bus services and found that we could use them in a couple of cases for travel in one direction. It meant that on those days we could double the distance walked on the official footpath, and this reduced the number of walks to about forty. I have described these, more or less, in the order that they were completed.

In reality we spread the Pennine Way walk over the greater part of two seasons, but we still managed to have a holiday each year in some other part of the U.K. Tackling the Pennine Way in this manner it was possible to defeat the real enemy—the weather. If the weather was too severe we didn't set out. There were two or three occasions when we started in rain that looked as if it might persist, but we never set out in bad visibility, and in the main we walked in good, dry weather.

We were not complete novices as far as walking was concerned. As campers, who had been converted to caravanning, we relished the outdoor life, and for the past six or seven years had developed our walks from four miles to in extreme cases, sixteen miles. We had from the start appreciated the need for good walking boots and sound waterproof clothing. As our walks had lengthened to more remote spots we had found a compass a great reassurance, even when it wasn't essential, and there is no substitute for an Ordinance Survey map, if possible and affordable a 1 to 25000.

For safety we always carry a whistle. The need for this was brought home to us whilst climbing Snowdon. A complete change in the weather from bright sunshine to hail, thunder and lightning, had caught many walkers on the summit. A nearby walker was a casualty. It was the only time we have heard the whistle being used to summon help, but we were amazed at its effectiveness.

One other very satisfying piece of equipment is my pedometer. It is nice to know how many miles have been covered, although our legs also pass this message. Over the years I have been able to measure distances fairly accurately using my pedometer, and the mileage quotes for the walks described were as registered, and not as measured on a map. The total mileage, covering all walks, was practically five hundred. It sounded a lot until a non-walking friend of mine said, "Over two years? That's less than a mile a day!"

We always carry our own food. We are picnic addicts. Three flasks of tea cover elevenses, lunch and afternoon break and it washes down our sandwiches. Fruit and a block of Kendal Mint Cake always helps. Because we like the countryside we always carry small field guides on birds and flowers, and we record all new

B.B. & E.M. on the Pennine Way.

discoveries. With a camera we store memories; we are not always looking for photographic studies but we do like to get shots of places that have some special significance.

Having completed all the walks we can assure anyone, especially of our age group, who completes the Pennine Way, that there is a wonderful feeling of satisfaction, and you will have been to many places that the vast majority of the population hardly know exist. But even if only odd walks are picked out there will be immense satisfaction in exploring this famous footpath.

Whether it be one walk or forty walks our wish for everyone is, "Have a pleasant journey."

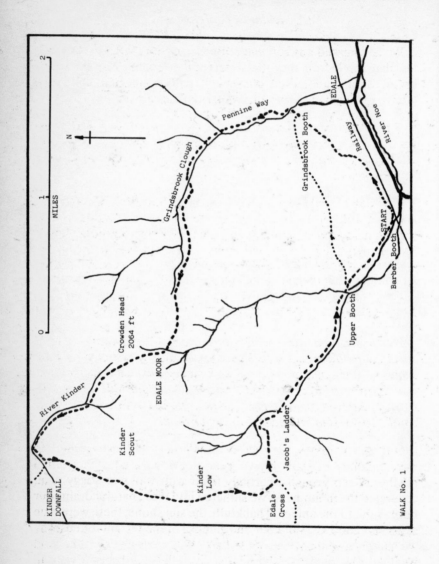

WALK No. 1

4

WALK 1
EDALE TO KINDER DOWNFALL

(A circular walk of nine miles)

We had parked our caravan at Barber Booth (MR 110/113847) less than a mile from the official start of the Pennine Way at Grinds-brook Booth, and, as a convenient path connected these two points, we decided to start our walk from the caravan.

A path crossed the railway line and then crossed the fields emerging by a campsite at Grindsbrook Booth. From there a sign indicated the path over a footbridge and up the valley to Grindsbrook Clough.

This was a very easy section as it passed through a wooded area and up a wide, green valley. The gradient increased and there were some outcrops of rock and then we entered Grindsbrook Clough. The path became rough and stony, and in places, followed the actual water course over a natural rock stairway. Looking back we could see Lose Hill and Whin Hill and, on reaching the edge of the plateau, grotesquely shaped, weather-worn rocks broke the skyline on either side.

Having crossed the Grindsbrook the left hand branch of the stream was followed on to the moor, and as the stream and the semblance of a path petered out we kept heading in a westerly direction, on a bearing of about 300 degrees. In about half a mile after leaving one water course another was reached which ran north to south. This was identified as Crowden Brook.

Our surroundings were an awe inspiring sight. All around us were mounds of dark brown peat, some covered with stunted heather. Deep groughs, partially filled with water or soggy peat, separated the mounds. As we slithered into these natural drains our boots sank to the ankles. Thankfully the sun shone, there were blue skies and good visibility but one glimpse of the terrain told us why we had been well advised not to tackle this crossing except in good weather. Our compass and map (1 to 25000 Dark Peak) were in constant use, but the twisting groughs, or hags, made straight line walking impossible. When on the mounds the surrounding vista appeared flat and unbroken with no useful landmarks, when in the depressions, nine or ten feet deep, nothing could be seen except the next crumbling slope.

We followed Crowden Brook to the north. The path was vague and, reaching the apparent source, we took a bearing of 335 degrees (25 degrees west of north) and headed for the Kinder River. This took us just to the south and west of Crowden Head, which at 2064 feet is the high spot of the moor. After about three-quarters of a mile we dropped into the wide water course of the Kinder River.

There is little real beauty on this wild moor, but we felt a sense of achievement as we scrambled in and out of the deep groughs. The sight of fellow walkers was encouraging but striking the Kinder River was truly exhilarating. The wet spongy peat had gone, the twisting, deep channel protected us from the breeze, the water's edge was firm and gritty and walking was easy. Following the gently flowing water through Kinder Gate we marvelled that such a small stream could have cut a passage through the rocks.

Kinder Downfall was a picture. The overnight rain had added a little to the flow of water, and the west wind snatched it as it tumbled over the rocks, and created a mist of white spray. If the weather had been drier the walk would have been easier but this beauty would have been missed.

Having followed the stream to the Downfall we turned towards the south, practically following the contours along the edge of the moor, and headed for the trig point of Kinder Low. From there, losing height and still heading south, the junction of paths at Edale Cross soon came into view.

This part of the walk showed two worlds. To our left the dark, satanic, peat moors, and to our right green fields, roads and villages, people and industry. Our path led over large mounds of loose peat which had the appearance of rich red-brown sand dunes, and shapeless footprints told of passing walkers.

At Edale Cross we turned left and followed a clear path, losing height constantly but dropping quickly when we reached Jacob's Ladder. We followed the rough path down the escarpment to the old bridge over the stream, and joined the wide cart track ahead.

The little stone bridge was a perfect picture in the sunshine. The clear water gurgled over stones, shining like jewels, and we sat and bathed our feet in the cool water. Part way down the valley was a National Park information room with photographs, charts and

Bliss, perfect bliss!

explanations, and swallows nesting in the rafters. A nearby house offered soft drinks and tea. This was back in civilisation.

The cart track led us to Upper Booth where signs guided us through the cluster of buildings. Our path led through the fields, and back to Barber Booth, but the alternative Pennine Way took the slightly higher ground back to Grindsbrook Booth, and the old Nag's Head Inn.

It was satisfying having completed our first stage of the Pennine Way. Our great adventure had begun with a modest walk full of variety. It had shown us bleakness and beauty, potential danger and absolute tranquility, it was a perfect introduction.

The next two sections were planned to start from the A57, the Snake Pass road, so Glossop seemed an obvious choice for a caravan park. We selected a site from the guide supplied by the Peak Park Planning, slightly to the west of Glossop.

It was dusk as we drove into the site. The sun and clear skies had changed to dull grey and threatening clouds, and the sky matched our spirits when we saw the proposed stopping place. Waist high stinging nettles surrounded deserted, dilapidated caravans. Unused toilets of rotting wood were collapsing into the surrounding rubbish. We found a clear spot, levelled the van and closed the door. We looked at each other and, in unison said, "In the morning we move."

7

The morning arrived, it didn't dawn! The skies were heavy, a slight drizzle misted the windows and the prospects didn't look good. We hitched up and, grudgingly, paid our dues, and headed for the A57. As our height increased the mist thickened and lights were necessary. We didn't even stop on reaching the spot where the Pennine Way crossed the road. Our waterproofs, our compass and our map were in the rucksack, but we were walking for pleasure, and only the fool-hardy wander on to the moors in bad visibility. We drove on to one of our favourite sites, at Youlgreave, and went for short walks in the beautiful Derbyshire Dales until the mist cleared from the crests of the surrounding hills.

The Camping and Caravanning Club, of which we are members, had a holiday site at Holmebridge, and that was an area that we knew and liked. We decided to move there and motor to the Pennine Way each day. There in the shadow of an old mill, and close to a friendly pub we found good, clean camping and pleasant company. It was agreed to make this our base for the next four walks.

KINDER DOWNFALL TO SNAKE PASS

(A circular walk of ten miles)

The first drive from the Holmebridge site was rather longer than would normally have been expected, but memories of our fruitless night's sleep in Glossop made it feel worthwhile. The sun had re-appeared and in glorious sunshine we climbed steeply up through the village of Holme and over Holme Moss. The Woodhead valley stretched before us and the road dropped quickly to skirt round the chain of reservoirs that seemed to fill the valley bottom. Crossing between the reservoirs, on the B6105, we saw back packers cross-ing the road at the start of their final stage of the north to south Pennine Way. Our road led to Glossop and then left up the A57; at the high point we saw the Pennine Way crossing but we continued on and down the hill to Birchin Clough Bridge (MR 110/110914). Starting the walk from this point meant that we split the stretch of road walking, and also that the finish would be on an easy downhill section.

Our original plan was to walk down the road, but in fact devious little paths existed in the narrow wooded area between the road and the river. We walked downstream and passed the point where the River Ashop flows down the clough, and the Snake Path descends. Continuing downstream to the next confluence, where Fairbrook joins the River Ashop, and crossing the river we proceeded up this valley with its rather steep sides. Several tracks existed, in places climbing the valley sides, but the brook was our guide, and we followed this, climbing quite steeply at times, for almost two miles.

In contrast to our previous, aborted, attempt everything went perfectly. The road traffic could hardly be heard as we strolled by the stream, as it bubbled down Lady Clough, and surrendered itself to River Ashop. The climb up Fairbrook was reasonably hard, but we were fresh and, once again, the sound of the small river, with its minor waterfalls and small secluded pools, was music to our ears. Heather clad slopes provided cover for red grouse which noisily flew away, skimming the bushes, as we approached. The occasional

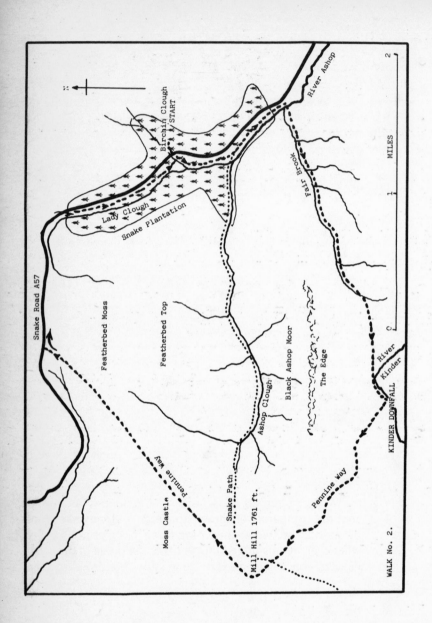

Snake Road A57

Birchin Clough
START

Lady Clough

Snake Plantation

River Ashop

Fair Brook

Featherbed Moss

Featherbed Top

Black Ashop Moor

The Edge

River
Kinder

KINDER DOWNFALL

Ashop Clough

Snake Path

Mill Hill 1761 ft.

Moss Castle

Pennine Way

Pennine Way

WALK No. 2.

0   1   2
MILES

backcap was perched on a gorse bush and proclaimed that this was his territory.

The track, which led up the valley, was heading a little south of west, and roughly followed the river, on a bearing that averaged about 250 degrees. As the ground levelled off the water course turned to the south, and we left the stream and headed due west. The terrain was rough, there was no discernible path, and the peat groughs seemed to run in all directions except west. After about half a mile, heading west, we dropped into the wide water course of the Kinder River and followed it to the Downfall.

The Kinder Gate grough, with its silver sand and loose stones, was certainly welcome after struggling over a pathless waste. It was like coming home to wander down to Kinder Downfall. In the sunshine walkers were everywhere, climbers were scrambling over the steep rock face, and the less energetic were sitting and watching. It was a natural place for our picnic.

At the Downfall we turned to the north west on a well-trodden path, keeping the triangulation point on our right. The path followed the contours with only a few minor ups and downs, with the Kinder Reservoir deep in the valley to our left. A short, sharp descent, followed by a gentle climb took us to Mill Hill (1761 ft). In that depression we had crossed the Snake Path. From this point the track closely followed the watershed heading north east, generally following the fence line. Keeping on the same bearing we crossed the Featherbed Moss and the path became more obvious as the A57 was approached.

Kinder Downfall to Mill Hill was a leisurely stroll along the top of the escarpment, but then we faced the moor again. By that time peat groughs were accepted as a way of life and we enjoyed the experience over Featherbed Moss, despite the conditions underfoot. At first the comparatively green appearance deceived us, but we soon found that we were squelching through a glutinous peaty mixture whenever we misjudged the width of the pools of brackish water that were concealed in every depression. We could see the traffic in the distance and were soon out on the busy tarmac road, trying to ignore the cars that lined the verges.

We turned right and followed this main road (A57) for about a mile before reaching a wooded section, where we left the road.

"Is this the featherbed?"

Following paths between the trees and heading downstream was a straight forward route back to our starting point.

The mile on the road was a respite for our weary legs, but petrol and diesel fumes made us long for the open moorland as hurrying motorists roared past. It was nice to get off the road and walk between the trees and by stream. The sun was still shining for our drive back to Holmebridge.

WALK 3
SNAKE PASS TO CROWDEN

(An out and home walk of fourteen miles)

We started our day with another pleasant drive over Holme Moss and down to Crowden. Passing the mast on the top of the hill there was no thought of how much we would use that landmark when crossing the moors. It was like the North Star, as it was only a couple of degrees off due north from our moorland high spot, Bleaklow Head. The little car park, near to Crowden Bridge, had only one other user, and we were soon on our way down the road on foot. One or two late risers were leaving the Youth Hostel, but none were going south.

Starting from the car park (MR 110/072992) we walked a short way in the direction of Stalybridge, crossed Crowden Bridge, and turned up a short walled track on our right. At the T junction on the track we turned left and, in a few yards, joined the Pennine Way. Continuing down the lane, and studying our map, we realised that we had left the official route, but as this was an out and home walk it wasn't important. Rejoining the main road and continuing westwards we saw the Pennine Way crossing, and went down the bank and over the dam head between Torside and Rhodeswood reservoirs. This brought us to the B6105 and the old railway crossing. Our path ran diagonally to our left, and then climbed steeply up the west side of Torside Clough.

The railway looked so forlorn, and yet a few years ago it appeared to be a busy link between Manchester and Sheffield. Looking back we saw the beauty of the valley, even if the reservoirs, the railway and the roads were man-made.

The path was quite distinct and easy to follow, running approximately parallel to the river, some four hundred feet below. Torside Castle was to our right, and the path crossed the stream to Jack Track Well.

Our path clung to the steep bank, with almost precipitous drops into the valley. Heather and short, bristle-like grass covered the steep slopes and, for a period the ubiquitous peat was missing. As the gradient lessened our track took us into the wet spongy moss,

13

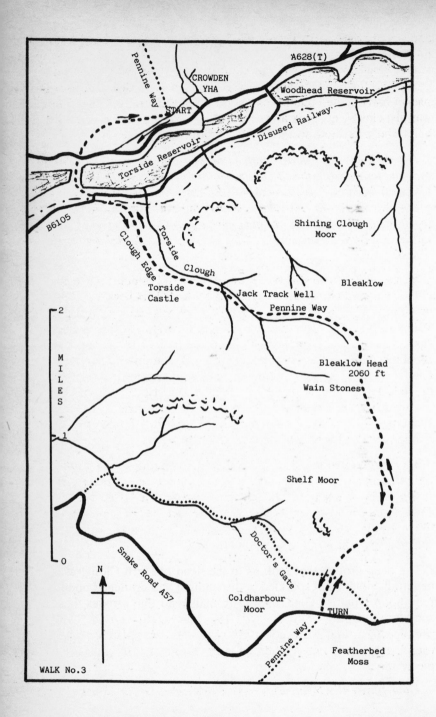

Pennine Way

A628(T)

CROWDEN
YHA

Woodhead Reservoir

START

Torside Reservoir

Disused Railway

B6105

Clough Edge

Torside
Clough

Shining Clough
Moor

Bleaklow

Torside
Castle

Jack Track Well
Pennine Way

2

M
I
L
E
S

1

Bleaklow Head
2060 ft

Wain Stones

Shelf Moor

Doctor's Gate

0

N

Snake Road A57

Coldharbour
Moor

TURN

Pennine Way

Featherbed
Moss

WALK No.3

14

and small trickles of water oozed out at every foot-tread, and joined the main stream.

Jack Track Well was a sheltered little depression with stone out-crops, and the main stream emerged from a narrow defile. A back-packer had decided that it was a good place to spend the night—he was just closing his pack as we arrived. He left, we sat down in this quiet, sheltered suntrap and had our morning cup of tea.

An obvious well trodden path ran alongside the small tributary that had joined from the east and we followed this path up Wildboar Grain. It became less distinct and the stream, which was turning south, was lost in the peat. We veered to the south, gaining height to reach Bleaklow Head. To confirm our position a bearing was taken on the trig point to the south, it was 195 degrees, and Holme Moss was due north.

We re-entered the world of peat groughs and doubt, when the path disappeared and our search for Bleaklow Head began. There didn't appear to be any true crest, and it was only the sight of the Wain Stones that truly confirmed our location. These weirdly shaped stones stood on a dry gravelly bed, a little to the south of Bleaklow Head. The terrain here was only slightly different to Kinder Scout. There was more vegetation, the bilberries were not in fruit, but the tough little bushes clothed most of the moor, and the groughs, cut by the water, seemed to be even deeper. Generally speaking, the ground was drier than we had encountered on Kinder, but our footprints rapidly filled with water.

We continued to the south and struck a deep grough with a sandy pathway, and followed this, bearing a little to the east in places, but in the main keeping south. Our path passed the head of Hern Clough, and went on to the slightly higher ground at Alport Low. We followed a vague track, on bearing 220 degrees, and headed for the moving traffic a mile ahead, on the A57.

The deep grough that took us to the head of Hern Clough was beautiful. Silver sand sparkled in the sunlight and crunched under-foot. Soon Doctor's Gate, the old Roman road that crosses these southern Pennines, was crossed. The busy traffic on the A57 rumbled past, and we went to the road and immediately turned round, and headed back to the moor to find a suitable, secluded, picnic spot.

The return walk, by the same route, was easier. We picked up our landmarks to Bleaklow Head. Wildboar Grain was 20 degrees west of north (just as stated by Tom Stephenson) and from there Jack Track Well was easily reached.

We stopped at the Wain Stones and tried, without success, to visualise the wind and weather worn sculpture of a kiss. From Bleaklow Head we looked south to Kinder, with a sense of satisfaction, and north to Holme Moss, with a feeling of confidence. Many more deep footprints, that filled with water, were made as we found our way to Wildboar Grain and the downhill path by the stream came as a relief. Reaching the confluence we once again stopped for a cup of tea, and wondered who created this strange sounding name, Jack Track Well.

The easy to follow path dropped back into Longendale and to Torside reservoir and crossed the busy A628. This time we followed the official route and went diagonally across two fields to High-stones, then dropped down to the small lane where the Pennine Way was first joined at the start of our walk.

The easy descent into Longdendale made a pleasant finish to our walk. The sun was still shining and the valley looked peaceful. The hills opposite seemed to be devoid of life, and we tried to visualise the problems that could lie in those barren heights, and our next instalment of the Pennine Way.

WALK 4

SADDLEWORTH ROAD (A635) TO CROWDEN

(A circular walk of thirteen miles)

It was decided to walk this section from the A635 walking the Pennine Way from north to south, then, having reached Crowden, a decision would be made whether to return by the same route or to make it a circular walk. Minor roads took us from Holmebridge to the A635, which we followed westwards towards Saddleworth. As the road levelled off on the crest of the hill, we saw the Pennine Way sign and a suitably wide verge for parking. The morning sun made the moor look attractive and we eagerly donned our packs.

We left the road at MR 110/052063 heading in a southerly direction, indicated by the sign, but could not truly recognise any path. The map indicated a bearing of 120 degrees and this was followed on a not very apparent watershed. Our track tended to vary direction slightly, either way, to avoid wet patches, There was still no path when, after about two miles, we saw the trig point on Black Hill slightly to our right.

The initial track passed through hummocky wet land with odd patches of white cotton grass, but round the trig point was dry and firm as we walked through crumbly peat. This spot is also known as Soldiers Lump, derived from the soldiers of the triangulation party that seemed to find the only truly dry spot on the entire moor. Several walkers were already there, having covered the five or six miles from the Crowden Youth Hostel. Greetings were exchanged, many of them were young enough to be our grandchildren, but all were doing the same thing, and there was the usual spirit of comradeship that is found all along the Pennine Way.

We turned right at Black Hill, on a wide, gently falling track over bare peat. The walking was easy, and the track appeared obvious, to the head of Crowden Great Brook. From there we followed on the right hand side of the river, generally maintaining our height, as the river dropped away in the valley. After about a mile the path drifted well clear of the river and climbed over Laddow Rocks, on a pleasant incline. Having passed the Rocks, and still on a distinct

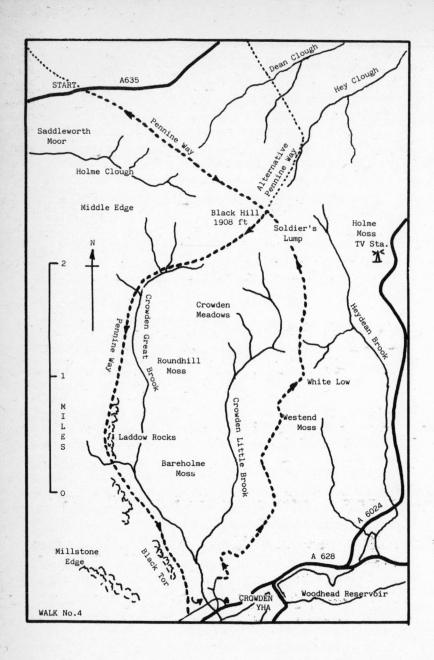

START

A635

Dean Clough

Hey Clough

Saddleworth
Moor

Pennine Way

Holme Clough

Alternative Pennine Way

Middle Edge

Black Hill
1908 ft

Soldier's
Lump

Holme
Moss
TV Sta.

N

2

Crowden
Meadows

Crowden Great Brook

Pennine Way

Roundhill
Moss

Heydean Brook

1

White Low

M
I
L
E
S

Crowden Little Brook

Laddow Rocks

Westend
Moss

0

Bareholme
Moss

A 6024

Millstone
Edge

Black Tor

A 628

CROWDEN
YHA

Woodhead Reservoir

WALK No.4

18

southerly course, the path dropped, sharply at first and then more gently, until the walled lane, above Crowden Bridge, where we started our previous walk, was reached.

The ground was dry and comparatively even as we left Black Hill, and it was a pleasant change from the rough terrain of some other moors. On reaching Crowden Great Brook the walk became more interesting, with more vegetation and variety in our surroundings on the climb to Laddow rocks. In places the path ran very close to the edge of these inland cliffs, and we could peer over the edge into a wide basin, with the river meandering southwards. The peaty moor was behind us and Crowden was scheduled for our lunchtime picnic.

On reaching the walled lane at Crowden we turned left towards the Youth Hostel, crossed the river and, at the cross roads, turned left again but then kept right at the fork. This led us in a zig-zag up a very steep hill between two disused quarries. A faint track up this steep hillside took us to the ridge of Hey Edge. The path ran almost due north to Westend Moss, and at the high point it turned slightly eastward, heading directly for the Holme Moss mast, on a bearing of 35 degrees, for about half a mile, to reach White Low. Following the watershed we turned north and picked up the trig point at Black Hill to our left.

The climb out of Longdendale was hard going and called for frequent rests, but each one presented a different view of the valley, and our surroundings were interesting. At the top of the climb it was not as barren as we had expected or had experienced on our previous walks. The mast at Holme Moss was a welcome companion for much of our return journey, and it was comforting to be able to tie up with an obvious and known landmark. Black Hill was deserted, the dark bare peat contrasted with the coarse, grey-green grass, but it was dry. It was easy to conjecture what this would be like in wet weather, and we were thankful that our crossing of this peaty moorland was in ideal conditions.

We left Black Hill on a bearing of about 240 degrees, following a vague path which quickly disappeared, but soon the road was visible, and a solitary parked car, which was our target, so we dispensed with the compass.

The return from Black Hill to the A635 was just a repeat of the morning, except that the sun had moved. We had taken eight hours to cover only thirteen miles, but we had enjoyed every minute of the day, after all, walking is for pleasure not just achievement.

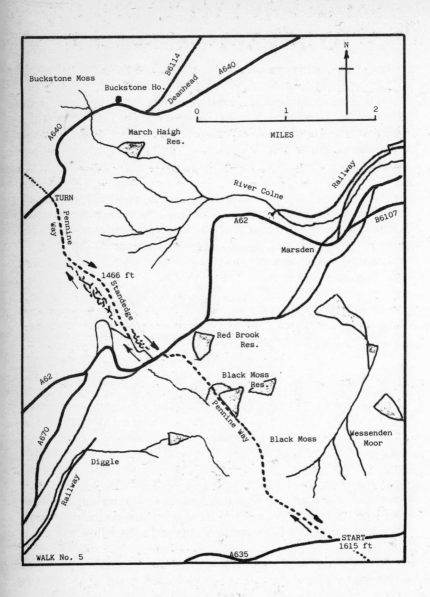

Buckstone Moss

Buckstone Ho.

B6114

Deanhead

A640

N

Buckstone Moss

A640

March Haigh Res.

0   1   2

MILES

River Colne

Railway

TURN

Pennine Way

A62

B6107

1466 ft

Standedge

Marsden

Red Brook Res.

Black Moss Res.

A62

Pennine Way

A670

Black Moss

Wessenden Moor

Diggle

Railway

START 1615 ft

WALK No. 5

A635

20

WALK 5

SADDLEWORTH ROAD (A635)
TO BUCKSTONES (A460)

(An out and home walk of twelve miles)

Still using the Holmebridge site we headed up for the same point of the A635 as on Walk four, and parked up. The skies were rather grey and the sun was totally obscured, but the weather was dry and the outlook reasonable. We still had no call to unpack our waterproofs.

The route was the continuation of our previous day's walk, starting at MR 110/052063, and following a path on a bearing of about 240 degrees. After about half a mile the track turned slightly more to the north, curving west again to pass over the dam head of Black Moss reservoir. It climbed slightly and then dropped down again to the Standedge cutting, with Redbrook reservoir to our right.

As we left the tarmac road on Saddleworth Moor there was a vague path which led us through hummocks of coarse grass, and shallow depressions which still held water, despite the fine weather. Chestnut palings, dead heather, old pallets and planks of wood had been used in an attempt to stabilise the path. Some of the deeper groughs had the usual floor of white sand, and these were used as paths wherever possible. Where the black peaty mud was exposed it contrasted vividly with the white cotton grass that seemed to thrive in these austere conditions. We didn't know where White Moss ended and Black Moss began, it all looked the same, but the reservoir provided a convenient halt. Squawking blackhead gulls and herring gulls, and a lonely pair of mallards were our only company. The road over Standedge, the A62, was no longer nose to tail with heavy wagons; most of these were now on the motorway, but there were still a fair number of cars and a few fellow walkers.

We crossed the A62 and a lane, opposite a parking area on the Manchester end of the cutting, took us back to the moor. A clear patch led in a generally north-westerly direction along the edge of the escarpment, and to the trig point on Millstone Edge. At the end of the rocks the path turned to the north over pleasant and dry

21

*moorland and took us to the next road which crosses the Pennines,
the A640, the Buckstones road.*

Regaining the moorland, after crossing the A62, we felt that the
really rough country was being left behind. The patch round the
rocks was dry and gravelly. There was a tablet, set in the rock, com-
memorating Ammon Wrigley, a poet who died in 1946. A little way
past that was a large flat rock, it was the perfect lookout spot, giving
a wide panoramic view of the lower, flatter land to the west of the
Pennines. With only a slight deterioration of the path we left the
outcrops of the rocks, and crossed grass and heather to reach the
A640, which was our turning point.

*The return journey was easy and straightforward, following exactly
the same path back to the A635.*

Going back we saw things from a different angle. The upper
Colne Valley, on our left, looked smoke free and peaceful, but it
reminded us of the Luddites who worked in the area during the
industrial revolution. They tried to stop progress and mechanisa-
tion, and had been unsuccessful, and the woollen industry had
prospered for three or four generations. But now many of the mills
were idle, their smoke stacks were cold, because the industry had
declined when progress and modernisation had not been main-
tained, and foreign competitors had stolen the markets.

The large white house on the A640, behind us and to our left,
held the secrets of an unsolved murder, and as our walk ended on
Saddleworth Moor, there were even more gruesome memories of
the moors murders, and the burial of young children only a mile or
so away. But these were mere drops in the ocean of time and did not
detract from the beauty of or surroundings.

We drove back to Holmebridge and, after a meal, prepared to
move. A drive down the valley, "The Last of the Summer Wine"
country, and through Huddersfield to Outlane on the A640.
Passing over the M62 the chosen site was on the left, in the village
of Outlane, which has now been swallowed by Huddersfield. The
M62 passed close by, but was unobtrusive and the setting was
pleasing. It wasn't a modern site, but it had good toilet facilities and
an unusual feature—baths, not showers. A nice, hot soak was
appreciated.

A640 BUCKSTONES TO A58 BLACKSTONE EDGE

(An out and home walk of eleven miles)

We left the Outlane site in bright sunshine heading for the hills, straight up the A640. The M62 ran close to our road and heavy goods vehicles could be seen roaring along and belching black smoke as they changed gear on the climb. Our road was quiet. Scammonden reservoir sparkled in the sunlight, and a continuous line of moving traffic crossed the dam head and disappeared into the cutting. We recognised our turning point of yesterday, and a nearby wide verge provided convenient parking.

Our walk started from MR 110/003123 on the A640, but in less than half a mile our path had taken us on to map 109. A Pennine Way signpost on the A640 indicated a distinct path heading north-west to White Hill. Near the summit it turned due west and passed the trig point. We then picked up our prime landmark, the Post Office mast on Windy Hill, and headed for it. The path passed just to the right of the mast, then across the A672 and on the impressive footbridge over the M62.

We had been warned of a wet passage on this walk but the fine weather of the past two weeks had drained away the water and the going was good. The trig point was on the watershed with streams forming nearby and running in several directions, but a little further on the path was of fine grit that formed the edge of the peat cap. A gentle decline towards the A672, with such an obvious landmark as the Post Office tower an aiming point, was a pleasant stroll, and there were no problems continuing to the M62. We paused on Ernest Marples' motorway bridge and watched the traffic passing below, feeling sorry for those people in their little tin boxes.

We crossed the footbridge and followed a path towards the west which soon veered northwards, on a bearing of about 30 degrees west of north, and climbed slightly. This indistinct, damp path led us to Blackstone Edge, in a little over a mile, after crossing the M62, and we then wended our way along the escarpment in a northerly direction. Leaving the rocks behind, we crossed the old Roman road

23

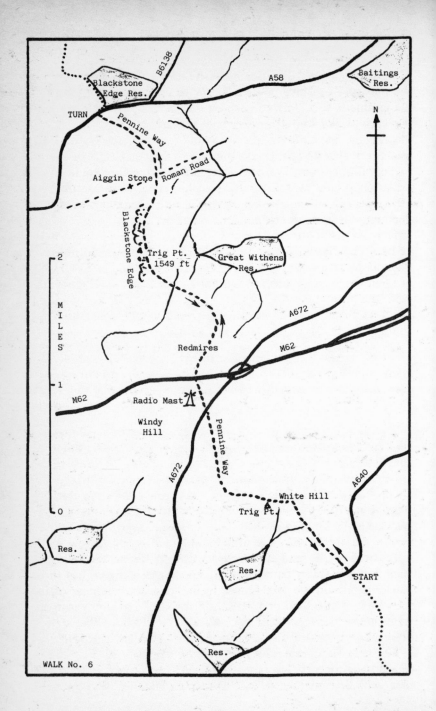

WALK No. 6

24

at Aiggin Stone, and continued northwards on a small path to the A58.

Immediately we crossed that stylish footbridge the land changed. We were on Red Mires. The path is vague and, even in dry weather, the ground is wet. This was back to the peat moor we knew from our early walks, but a passing walker, heading south, told us that this was the last until the Cheviots were reached. Blackstone Edge was not new to us, but it was still impressive. Vast weather carved rocks, with smooth curves and gritty surfaces surrounded us. There was a panorama of industrial Lancashire and, between conurbations, green fields and a few trees. The trees were special on the Pennine Way; so far there had been very few.

The Aiggin Stone, on the Roman Road, had some faint, indecipherable markings, and although previously we had seen it recumbent, it now stood proudly erect. Beyond, our track passed through more rough heather and furze on peaty soil. Reaching the A58, our turning point, we went to the nearby White House Inn, just to confirm that civilisation still existed, and to check where we could park the car for the subsequent walk.

On the return a slight detour was made which followed a man-made watercourse from the A58, slightly to the west of the official path, and turned up the Roman road until we reached the Aiggin Stone. From there we retraced our morning walk.

It was on the Roman road that we met a walker with a map and a "Wainwright's Pennine Way Companion". He complained that the guide was too childishly simple for adult walkers. We watched him as he turned south, in the wrong place, and disappeared from view. He probably ended up in Rochdale! We wondered who was simple. Blackstone Edge was a rest point from which we tried to spot Lancashire landmarks before, reluctantly, picking up the track back to the peat of Red Mires. In hilly country we accept out and home walks because the land in reverse looks so different, but the drawback is that a sticky patch, discovered on the way out, has to be tackled again on the way home. In this case the wildness of the scenery was adequate compensation for this. Looking down the valley there were so many things and views that we had missed before that we passed through Red Mires with never a thought.

We were lucky, we had fine weather. In bad weather this is treacherous country. The entire walk was around the 1500 feet contour, which is frequently mist shrouded and wet which creates problems, although there is only about one hundred feet between the high and low points of the walk, which means that there is no strenuous climbing. Our walk had been very easy.

Then it was back to the caravan. There seemed to be a change in the weather, but that had to be expected. It was Friday evening, and the Spring Bank Holiday weekend was about to start. Saturday was planned for a walk to Stoodley Pike, Sunday was to be a shorter walk round Hebden Bridge, and on Monday our son had offered transport, so we planned to have a long walk to Cowling. As the sun set piercing rays found gaps in the dark clouds and, with some apprehension we prayed for a fine weekend.

WALK 7
A58 BLACKSTONE EDGE
TO STOODLEY PIKE
(An out and home walk of eleven miles)

A dull overcast morning greeted us when we opened the caravan door, wet grass and puddles of water told us that it had rained during the night, and we just hoped that it wasn't going to return for this holiday weekend. Having formerly lived in the Huddersfield area the small by-roads that run from Outlane, through Barkisland to Ripponden, and the A58 were known, and it was a relatively fast run to Blackstone Edge. The cloud was low but visibility was quite good, and there was the hope that the strong south-westerly breeze would keep the rain away. Parking was easy and signs, with the carved acorn, told us where the path crossed the road. (MR 109/968179).

A waterworks road led northwards and the Pennine Way followed this to Blackstone Edge reservoir, keeping to this distinct good path and heading slightly west of north. Two further reservoirs, Light Hazzles and Warland, were passed and the track turned north and then east for a short distance, but we soon spotted Stoodley Pike and kept heading in that general direction.

This was easy walking, certainly the easiest yet, the path was ideal. Looking out over Lancashire we could see Hollingworth Lake, and Rochdale beyond, with glimpses of coaches and cars hurtling towards the coast, and the promenade at Blackpool. Thousands of people would crowd on to the seafront for this general holiday, and up here there was not another living soul in sight. The path changed as we left the reservoirs but was still good, firm and distinct. Stoodley Pike was temptingly ahead, and such a landmark gave comfort, but it didn't seem to get any closer! A paved path led down to the Youth Hostel at Mankinholes, and we had the perfect view of the valley that stretches from Todmorden to Hebden Bridge and Calderdale.

Close up the Pike appeared massive. We entered a dark, dungeon-like room on the left and quickly retreated from the malodorous stench of a sheeps' toilet. The overnight rain had drained in from the surrounding moor and stones stood out like

27

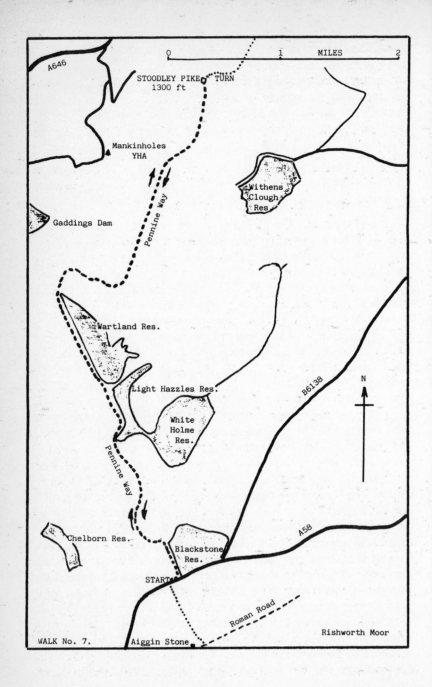

STOODLEY PIKE TURN
1300 ft

A646

Mankinholes
YHA

Pennine Way

Gaddings Dam

Withens
Clough
Res.

Wartland Res.

Light Hazzles Res.

White
Holme
Res.

B6138

N

Pennine Way

Chelborn Res.

Blackstone
Res.

START

A58

0   1   MILES   2

WALK No. 7.   Aiggin Stone   Roman Road   Rishworth Moor

28

small islands in a sea of dirty, green liquid. Balancing on similar stones in another doorway enabled us to reach stone steps that spiralled to a balcony, and we looked north to the walks ahead. It was a different country. There were stone walls, fields and houses, and heavy black clouds on the horizon. In the valley, almost under our feet, was the jumble of houses and factories of discoloured Yorkshire stone that was Hebden Bridge. The lowering sky threatened rain, so it was back to the moor for a quick picnic and the return walk.

The homeward journey was over exactly the same paths as the outward walk and no landmarks were necessary. Our target was the car park and the White House Inn on the A58.

Passing the reservoirs on the way back to the car we watched the gulls as they played in the wind, screaming at each other. An old saying stated that gulls inland was a sign of a storm. We forgot the dark skies that were billowing in from Lancashire and ignored the gulls, assuring ourselves that gulls were everywhere, and it was an old wives' tale. We were back at the car early. Why shouldn't we have an early finish? It's a holiday weekend!

There was an interesting sequel to our visit to Stoodley Pike. I had been unable to get a photograph when we walked there, but several weeks later, while passing nearby I decided to rectify this omission. An unclassified road from Mytholmroyd and Crag Vale goes to Withens Clough reservoir; from there a walk of a little over a mile would take me to Stoodley Pike. Parking at the nearest point I climbed the fairly steep slope, with no identifiable path towards the Pike. The skies gradually darkened and rain threatened as the summit was reached. Approaching the Pike I subconsciously noted that my path was on an extended diagonal of the square tower. I then walked round the tower looking for a decent background to the photograph. A sudden thick damp mist closed in, and the picture was hurriedly taken, without any discernible background, and tracks were made back to the car. All four corners of the tower looked the same, and visibility was down to twenty yards and decreasing. I turned my back to a corner and headed for the stile, I thought—I was wrong. This unseen path was descending rapidly with no stile or intervening stone wall. I hadn't my compass or map with me. Not needed, I thought, for such a short trip. I groped around in visibility which was down to a few feet, and eventually returned to the huge stone tower. I found the opening to the spiral staircase and climbed to the balcony, and stood at each corner in turn, waiting to see slight breaks in the swirling mist that would allow me to see a path to the stile.

Eventually I got my bearings, and found the stile, and struggled through gorse and heather towards Withens Clough reservoir. Lower down the hill the mist cleared and I saw that I would have missed the car by several hundred yards if the poor visibility had persisted. The experience re-emphasised the rule—on the Pennines always have a compass, a map, a whistle and a torch.

STOODLEY PIKE TO COLDEN

(A circular walk of ten miles)

Spring Bank Holiday Sunday, a day to remember! As we opened the caravan door heavy rain gusted in. Breakfast was consumed trying to see through heavily misted windows, with streaming water cascading down the glass. Cars hurtled along the M62 in clouds of spray. The question was—should we go walking? It was only a short stretch, but tomorrow was a long one to Cowling. To combine the two was too much, to reject free transport on Holiday Monday was unthinkable. "Perhaps it'll stop." was the optimistic comment, "and we have waterproofs." The decision was made! Through Holywell Green and Greetland to Halifax, and on to Hebden Bridge. The car was parked in a deserted car park (MR 103/992237) in the centre of the town and, in teeming rain, our waterproofs were donned and our walk started.

The car park was on the north side of the main through road (A646), we crossed to the south and, heading west, soon reached the bridge over the River Calder. This unclassified road, running first to the southwest but swinging finally southeast, led uphill. We turned left on a track at Erringden Grange and after about a mile there was a minor cross roads, but our track continued for five or six hundred yards to a point where the Pennine Way crossed. The Way went obliquely to our left, heading initially almost south, but then veering to cross a stile and up the climb to Stoodley Pike.

Despite the late start, and the fact that it was a general holiday, there was no sign of life in the town. The roads were shining wet, the gutters were full to overflowing, and the river was an angry, brown torrent, as it rushed under the bridge. The railway, road and river were all crowded into this narrow gorge. Houses and factories were crushed together and, in this dismal weather they all looked dead. We left the railway behind and entered Callis Wood. Under normal weather conditions this would have been a pleasant lane. In the heavy rain the trees broke the force of the weather but large drops splashed down from the water-laden leaves and almost invariably found a small gap between waterproof and body. We tried to think of sunny Bank Holidays and glorious sunshine, and plodded on. As we emerged on a narrow lane it was more exposed and the rain beat

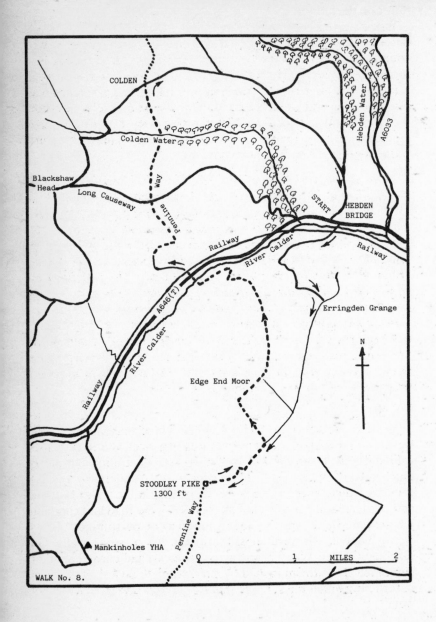

COLDEN

Colden Water

Blackshaw
Head

Long Causeway

Hebden Water

A6033

START

HEBDEN
BRIDGE

Pennine Way

Railway

River Calder

Railway

A646(T)

River Calder

Railway

Erringden Grange

N

Edge End Moor

STOODLEY PIKE
1300 ft

Pennine Way

Mankinholes YHA

0   1   MILES   2

WALK No. 8.

32

almost horizontally, urging us to reach shelter in the gaunt, grey tower on the hilltop.

When we reached the tower we found that visibility was good, despite the rain, and we could see two or three miles of wet countryside. Shelter was required. In desperation the dungeon-like room on the west side was targeted. The resident sheep were expelled, but after two or three minutes the remaining stench was overpowering and we retreated to the fresh air, and told the sheep that they could go back. The sheltered side of the tower provided a modicum of cover, and there we ate our soggy sandwiches, and warmed ourselves with a cup of hot tea.

We used the same path to leave Stoodley Pike, heading downhill and crossing a stile in the stone wall. The path turned left by the wall to the track that skirted Edge Moor and then led down to the main road (A646), the railway, the river and the canal. We crossed the road and followed a lane almost opposite under the railway line. The lane climbed steeply, round an old cemetery and a chapel, Mount Olive Baptist, zig-zagging up the hillside. The path involved farm roads, and following, or passing through, walls or stiles, but was distinct and easy to follow, with footpath signs in several places.

In comparatively open country the tarmac road, the Long Causeway, was crossed, and then the path dropped down to Colden Water. The bridge was crossed and another slope climbed to reach another tarmac road, with a scattering of houses. This was Colden, the point where we would leave the Pennine Way.

Leaving the tower and going downhill the weather seemed to deteriorate even further. Vicious squalls swept in from the southwest, and trickles of water were spreading from the neck waistwards. The waterproofs were resisting any penetration but damp patches were obviously being created in our underwear by this trickling water. There was a wooded section, in the valley bottom, and this gave some respite, but after crossing the road and climbing up the lane there was the added problem of perspiration. Rests were frequent, whenever possible in the lee of stone walls. On reaching Colden Water it was agreed that we had earned another cup of tea. The stream rushed by, pretending to be a river, and we, in turn, pretended the sun was shining and our underwear was not wet.

Our route was to the right at Colden via the tarmac road to Hebden Bridge, passing through Slack and Heptonstall. We picked our way through the small streets to the car to finish our first wet walk.

If the weather had been better the older houses of Colden could have been enjoyed. Many of them are old weavers' cottages and the upper windows are arranged to give some natural light for the weaver to thread up his loom, and to weave the heavy twill cloths, such as moleskins, that this area specialised in. The tarmac was hard underfoot, but the going was easy. The gradual decline increased after Heptonstall and our speed quickened as we were anxious to get dry, but Hardcastle Crags and Heptonstall warrant a further visit.

It was the first time, in this series of walks, that we had to cape up, and although the material in our waterproof clothing had resisted penetration we were still wet. Getting back to the caravan we were thankful for our independence. Our wet clothes were discarded and dry, warm ones were donned. A hot meal was prepared and whilst it was cooking we each had a hot bath. A large, laundry type tumble dryer in the gent's washroom intrigued me. There was a money slot, but a fellow camper assured me that coins weren't needed, and he pressed a switch to prove it. The large drum noisily rotated, and I had visions of an abundance of dry clothing.

I returned to the caravan, imparted the good tidings and collected everything together—the damp, the wet and the very wet, then trotted back to the washroom with a bulging plastic bag. Everything went in, the old machine clanked and groaned, and our clothes tumbled merrily. I gleefully returned to the caravan and ate a hearty dinner, listened to the news and then went to collect my dry clothes. As soon as I went in I sensed that something was wrong. I felt the glass panel in the door of the machine—it was ice cold. I opened the door and felt my clothes. Everything was wet, the damp ones were wet, the wet ones were wet and the very wet ones were still very wet.

My conscience pricked me. So I put twenty pence into the machine, on the assumption that one had to buy heat, switched on and made a wish. After a few minutes it was apparent that I had just wasted twenty pence.

The wet clothes were stuffed back into the plastic bag and we dashed around Huddersfield looking for a launderette. A nearby one had a notice "Sorry, closed Bank Holiday Sunday!" The town centre one was closed with no apologies. We went to the other side of town. There the notice said "We close at 8.00" it was five past eight.

We went back to the caravan. With the heater at full blast garments were dangled in front of the heater, and all around the interior of the van. The temperature rose, condensation poured off the walls and windows, but eventually everthing was dry. Our Spring Bank Holiday Sunday was over—and so to bed!

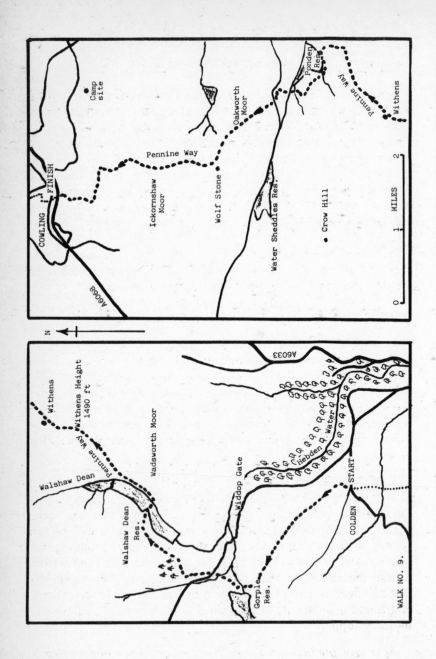

WALK 9
COLDEN TO COWLING
(A one way walk of fifteen miles)

Spring Bank Holiday Monday, sunshine streamed through the windows of the 'van, clear blue skies had replaced the clouds, and a slight northeast breeze gave a pleasant early morning nip to the air. A smoke-free, clean-looking Huddersfield, with idle factories, lay in the valley. In the distance the Emley Moor television mast was silhouetted against clear sky. A long walk of about fifteen miles was planned and we were to be met at Cowling at about 6.00 pm. Walking over open and often rough country, our estimate is two miles per hour, plus one hour for eating and drinking, so our start had to be no later than 9.30 am.

The same route to Hebden Bridge was followed, and the compulsory over-run to the turning point made, then back a couple of hundred yards to the road on our left to Heptonstall. There was plenty of space for parking near the fork for Widdop Moor (MR 103/978288) and we were ahead of schedule.

We took the road to Colden village and at the sign turned right, crossing a field and a track, and out on to the moor. The path was easy to follow, and surprisingly dry. It gradually backed to the northwest with the trig point half a mile to the south. Meeting a track from the south we turned north and crossed the reservoir outflow, and reached the Widdop Moor road. After a few yards on the road we turned right, at the Pennine Way sign, and headed for Walshaw Dean reservoirs.

The moors being crossed were certainly different to the wild peat moors of Kinder or Black Hill. Rough grass, in large tussocks, was interspersed with heather and gorse, and among this was some slightly squelchy peat which oozed water under our boots. The sun shone, skylarks soared into the sky, bees buzzed among the heather, and the air was full of music. After the initial climb from Colden the walking was easy. We skirted along one of the reservoirs that had been constructed on the upper reaches of Hebden Water, and found a sheltered, sunny spot on the dam head to have our morning cuppa.

After crossing between the first and second reservoirs we turned left by the stone built channel and, about half way along this reservoir, bore off to the right. The track led us to Withen Heights, a little over a mile away. Our path continued, passing Withins House, with its tablet about Wuthering Heights, and continued in a northeast direction, keeping to the main track and ignoring minor footpaths leading towards Haworth. The track became a lane at Master Stones and after another four or five hundred yards we turned left to Ponden Reservoir. Reaching the reservoir it was left again, round the south and southeast bank, to reach the road.

The view of the valley from Withens was in complete contrast to the Calder Valley at Hebden Bridge. Withens looked down into a wide, gentle, almost deserted valley, whereas Calderdale was narrow, congested and, at one time, highly industrial, with buildings crammed into every available space. On this stretch the path in many places was bare earth as a result of the thousands of feet that made the Bronte pilgrimage. The gentle slopes of the moor were clothed in springy, green turf, with a sprinkling of yellow flowering gorse bushes. The remains of Withens looked peaceful in the sunshine of Monday, but in the rain of Sunday it would have been a desolate lonely place. One or two fellow walkers, in boots and breeches, were on our track, but most of the people we met, on this stretch were in more traditional leisure clothes. They had left their cars and coaches in Haworth and were delicately picking their way round any rougher patches.

Our route crossed the Colne/Haworth road and climbed a field to reach another road, which looped round to our left, and then our path went off to the right and on to Oakworth Moor, heading for the high spot known as Bare Hill. The path turned towards the north over Ickornshaw Moor, and then dropped down towards Cowling. The direction remained fairly constant and for short stretches we were on either cart tracks or walled lanes. The finish was a fairly steep descent, through a field, to the Black Bull at Cowling.

Feeling that we were well up on our schedule we dawdled a little round the Ponden area. Ponden Hall appeared to be a hive of activity. The old seventeenth century house was making the most of the sunny bank holiday and was busy providing refreshments. We sought solitude and moved a little further, and sat near the reservoir and had our picnic. On Oaksworth moor we couldn't resist the urge to go to the trig point near Wolf Stones, and look out over the quiet countryside.

Ickornshaw Moor was peaty, and the path was breaking up rather badly. Some authority had laid chestnut palings which had bedded in and made the ground firm underfoot. A little workman's hut (the hut was small, not the workman) was still in place. Once again we thought of yesterday. It was easy to assess how welcome that hut would have been to anyone on this moor in that torrential rain. Shooting butts and summer houses became prevalent as the path dropped towards Cowling, and soon we saw two people approaching. The family had arrived, and our transport was waiting. Our legs said rest, our watch said 5.30 and our stomachs said eat.

That evening we made ourselves presentable and had dinner at a hotel. The map showed that we had covered about sixty miles of the Pennine Way, and in all, over one hundred miles had been walked. It called for a little celebration.

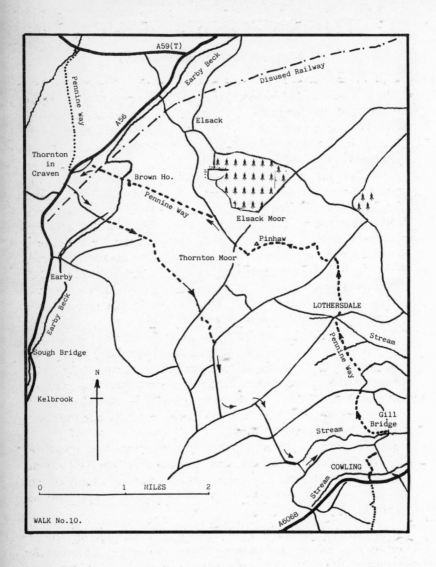

A59(T)

Earby Beck

Disused Railway

Pennine Way

A56

Elsack

Thornton
in
Craven

Brown Ho.

Pennine Way

Elsack Moor

Thornton Moor

Pinhaw

Earby

LOTHERSDALE

Earby Beck

Stream

Pennine Way

Sough Bridge

N

Kelbrook

Stream

Gill
Bridge

0   1   MILES   2

Stream

COWLING

WALK No.10.

Stream

A6068

40

WALK 10

COWLING TO THORNTON-IN-CRAVEN

(A circular walk of fourteen miles)

We had arranged to have a rest from the Pennine Way following the Spring Bank Holiday, and to pick up the threads of normal life. So on Tuesday it was a leisurely drive home. Later in the month we once again got the urge and headed north and picked up the Pennine Way in the village of Cowling.

The Camping and Caravanning Club have a list of Hideaway sites. These are, in the main, remote sites with no facilities other than water and waste disposal. The locations are often in farmer's field, with only one or two users at any one time, and such sites can be difficult to find. The site at Cowling was especially so because the wrong map references had been given. This meant that I took the caravan down a narrow farm lane, with high banks on either side, expecting to find an attractive remote site. All I found was two cottages and a dead end, which called for an unhitch, manual turn around, in a very restricted area, and another search.

When the site was found it was a beautiful spot, with a wonderful view over the valley, and only about a mile from the Pennine Way. Approaching the field via the farmyard, on a narrow, sludgy path, through a widespread manure heap was a minus mark, but after the soft peat of Kinder Scout it could be ignored. We settled in, had a lazy evening, watched the sun drop behind the hills, and prepared for an early start in the morning.

A quick run to the Black Bull and a convenient parking spot (MR 103/966530) in the morning, and our next stretch of the Pennine Way was started. This was a different environment to any of our previous walks. It seemed strange to be among houses and on farmland.

Our path led out of the Black Bull car park and past the school, and on to a minor road running almost due north. Reaching the stream at Gill Bridge we crossed to the north bank, passed by an old mill and then through a stile. Still in a northerly direction we climbed Cowling Hill, and took the steep downhill road opposite. The road turned sharply left and then right and our path left the

41

*tarmac at this second corner and dropped down to cross the beck,
and then climbed up towards Lothersdale. In the village we turned
right past the Hare and Hounds, and left at the Pennine Way sign.
This took us through a farmyard to a lane. At the end of the lane a
field path went due north, and parallel to a small stream on our
right. We crossed a tarmac lane near Kirk Sykes Farm, and headed
for Pinhaw Beacon. A wide green track, through deep heather,
headed southwest, for a short distance, and led to an old cart track.
We turned right and met the tarmac road at a three lane junction.
Taking the road opposite, and heading towards Elsack for about
half a mile, we picked up a path on our left, and crossed more fields,
using gates and stiles, mainly on a bearing of 300 degrees (almost
northwest), until we picked up a track leading to Brown House. This
path crossed Earby Beck, and the old railway track, and then took
the left fork to the main road, the A56.*

This part of the Pennine Way, was such a vast change from the
earlier parts that we constantly felt that we were trespassing.
Passing through pasture land, with animals grazing, and with
nearby farmhouses and buildings, we anticipated being stopped
and rebuked for invading property. This was no longer a holiday
period, it was late June, and only pensioners were on vacation, so
walkers were few and far between. The countryside was lush and
green, unlike the peat moors, and it seemed that the terrain was no
longer in opposition.

A house at the start of a path that led into Lothersdale had a
"Pennine Way Walkers Welcome" sign, and the Pennine Way sign in
the village confirmed that we were on the right track. Despite the
gentle nature of the countryside, there seemed to be more climbing
here than when we were on the moors. The path went up and down,
twisted in and out, gates had to be opened, and closed, stiles had to
be climbed—but there were no peat bogs. We were in civilisation
and couldn't decide whether it was an improvement or not.

*We turned left on the A56 and were anxious to leave this busy
road. Our chosen path was left again, down a small lane to Booth
Bridge, to pick up a small path running southeast to a lane, about
half a mile distant. An unfenced lane was almost opposite and this
was followed for a couple of hundred yards, until we reached the
buildings. The footpath was on the right, immediately after the
entrance to some dog kennels, and led across the small valley and
stream, to link up with Lane, which in turn, led to a tarmac road.
Almost opposite was another farm track and, at the end, a small*

footpath on our right took us to another minor road. We headed south, ignoring a lane doubling back on our left, then took the left fork at the T junction and turned left on the Lothersdale road. After about six hundred yards we went right, down a steep hill, straight across near a telephone box, and carried on to the next T junction. The road on our left took us back to Gill Bridge, and into Cowling.

The return route was pleasant but unexciting. The countryside had a gentle atmosphere, and the network of minor roads that we were forced to cross, were almost devoid of traffic. The footpath near the dog kennels was rather obscure, and an approach was made to the nearby house to ask for directions. An excited lady ordered me off her drive, swearing that my intrusion could cause her bitch to have stillborn pups. We longed for the open moors, and the courtesy of fellow walkers. The sky clouded over, and the unpleasant attitude of the "dog-lady" had depressed us. It was almost a relief to reach Cowling knowing that we were moving on.

"Geroff my land!"

We had our meal, tidied up and moved to Gargrave. It was a pleasant site, by the canal, and very near the village centre.

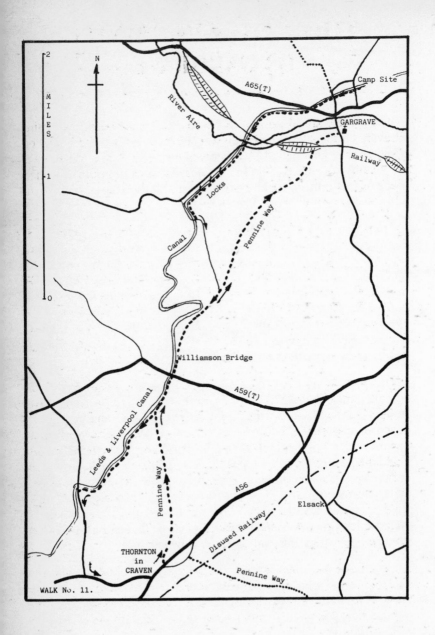

WALK No. 11.

44

WALK 11

THORNTON-IN-CRAVEN
TO GARGRAVE

(A circular walk of fourteen miles)

It is always an advantage to be able to leave the car with the caravan, on the site. We did this at Gargrave and had the bonus of being on the canal bank for the start of our walk. There was quite a bit of activity around the locks, and our walking boots and breeches made us feel rather gauche among the sun-tanned legs, brief shorts and soft shoes of the boating fraternity.

From the site (MR 103/935546) we followed the tow path of the Leeds Liverpool canal in a west or southwesterly direction, passing under the railway line, and on to the next set of locks. There our path turned south and left the canal, cutting off a large bend. This lane later joined up with the canal near the A59 crossing, and our path then went back to the tow path for almost two miles. We climbed back to a minor road at South Field Bridge and headed south to the T junction with the B6252. Left on the B6252 and left again on the A56 and the Pennine Way crossing was reached.

The walk along the canal towpath, and on a quiet country lane was easy and relaxing, but so much life around us felt strange. We stopped on the narrow lane, away from the canal and people, to have our cup of tea. It was on a slight rise and there were gorse bushes with bright golden flowers, birds sang and grasshoppers made their funny grating noise. The towpath between the A59 and the minor road was quieter and more tranquil. Only two narrow boats, chugging along the canal, invaded the serenity, but there were plenty of moorhens and coots bobbing about, and a pair of majestic looking swans. The village green at Thornton-in-Craven was our picnic location, watching the world go by.

Cam Lane leads north from the village green, and we followed this pleasant shady lane until it became a track leading to Langber Farm. A footpath on our right took us to the canal towpath, near the A59 at East Marton. Having passed under the A59 we carried on past Williamson Bridge and in about four hundred yards, left the towpath for a short stretch, cutting off a small bend, but rejoined the

45

lane, which we had used on our outward trip, for a further quarter of a mile in a northeasterly direction. This was followed by field paths in the same direction, as the lane swung away to our left. We crossed the railway near the east end of the cutting, and went diagonally across the field towards the church. There we joined a minor road into Gargrave which crossed over the river, and the canal, to the A65. A road on the left took us to the caravan site.

The return journey was quieter than the outward trip. Gentle walking through mildly rolling country would describe it. We noticed particularly the old double bridge that carried the A59 over the canal, and wondered why it hadn't been noticed on the way south. There were various reasons proffered for this strange bridge construction, but Wainwright's seems to be the most logical. He says that a severe dip was taken out of the road when motor traffic superseded the horse and cart, and the easiest way to do this was to build a bridge on a bridge. Fields, hedges, stiles and gates, grazing cattle and grassy lanes, are the prime memories of this part of the Pennine Way. All this coupled with long stretches of the Leeds to Liverpool canal gave us a very tranquil walk.

GARGRAVE TO MALHAM TARN

(A walk, mainly one way, of thirteen miles)

A short chat with the site proprietor about our desire to walk as much of the Pennine Way as possible, each day, brought the suggestion that, in this case, public transport could be used to get back to the site. He explained that a bus ran from Malham to Gargrave, and he even found out the times of the service. This meant that we could lengthen the day's walk and probably save a day.

Our walk, once again, started at the site (MR 103/935546) by taking the road opposite the gate to the T junction. The tarmac road then turned left but we turned right up a walled lane. Just past a small wood, on our right, we picked up a field path that climbed over Eshton Moor. This passed about three hundred yards east of the trig point, and struck the minor road over the River Aire at the northern end of the moor. We crossed the footbridge and walked on the west bank of the river to the next minor road, near Newfield Hall. This road was used to cross to the east bank of the river, and we followed the river upstream to the road crossing at Airton and then on to Hanlith. At Hanlith the route was along the road for a little way, up the hill and then dropping off to the left at a sharp bend, and heading back to the river and a weir. Near there the river forked, the stream to the east was ignored, as this lead to Gordale Scar, and we kept heading north to Malham.

This section of the walk was a complete holiday. The terrain made easy travel, only two or three other people were sharing the quietude, the weather was warm and sunny and the birds sang. As we walked through clumps of fern-like herbs the air was filled with pleasant, aromatic scents. We saw canterbury bells, blue cranesbill and musk, and we drank our morning tea sitting by a still pool and watched the trout jumping for files. A dipper, with his white breast-plate, bobbed from stone to stone as the water gurgled into the pool, and grey wagtails with yellow breasts helped their pied cousins to hunt insects. An old mill nearby had been converted into flats, and looked out over the river, but there was no sign of life. Further on, to our left, was the church of Kirkby Malham, but we had decided not to make any detours on this journey.

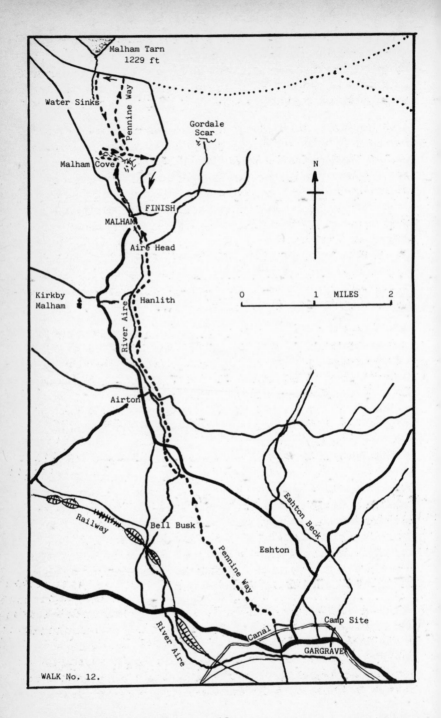

Malham Tarn
1229 ft

Water Sinks

Pennine Way

Gordale
Scar

N

Malham Cove

FINISH

MALHAM

Aire Head

Kirkby
Malham

Hanlith

River Aire

0   1   MILES   2

Airton

Railway

Bell Busk

Eshton Beck

Pennine Way

Eshton

Camp Site

River Aire

Canal

GARGRAVE

WALK No. 12.

48

Even in mid-week, in non-holiday period, there was quite a lot of activity in Malham. A little cafe on our left was serving lunches. We refrained, but dared to spoil our picnic lunch by having an ice cream. Ducks paddled in the stream, and begged for scraps from the picnickers in the village centre.

We took the minor road on the left from the village centre, immediately before the bridge, and followed walkers and trippers towards Malham Cove. After about half a mile on the road, a sign marked the way to the base of the rock face, and a path went down to the river and followed the bank to where the water emerged from a small cave, at the foot of the cliff. A distinct, man-made path with steps, to the left of the bare limestone, led to the top of the Cove, and over a stile. Then heading almost west, along the top of the cliff, we scrambled over huge limestone blocks. We passed the dry valley on our left, and over another stile. Our path then swung to the north and crossed Prior Rakes to an unfenced road which was on the south side of Malham Tarn.

Malham Cove really is something special! This was not our first visit to Malham, but it was the first time that we had walked up to the low arch at the base of the cliff that is considered by many to be the birth place of the River Aire. This is not so; at this point the River Aire is flowing underground and emerges lower down the valley. We found a warm, sheltered rock, with a flat table-like surface, on which to have our picnic, before tackling the steep climb that was ahead of us.

The view from the top of the Cove was fantastic, but it wasn't as surprising as the rock formation over the Cove. The limestone blocks resembled overgrown paving stones, almost reminiscent of the Giant's Causeway. Ferns grew out of some of the crevices and, here and there, small bushes and stunted trees were trying to get a foothold. Care was needed when crossing this section as an unseen crevice could mean a sprained ankle. We glanced up the dry river bed which, in the distant past, carried the River Aire, and we knew that that was a topic for the return journey.

Having reached the tarmac road we turned left to the gate where the stream crossed the road, and followed a vague path over the turf to the south. This led to Water Sinks, where the water disappeared into the rocky stream bed. We headed southwest. After about a quarter of a mile our path came to the head of the dry valley. This led us back to the limestone "pavement" overlooking the Cove. We turned east, over the high stile, and then in a southeast direction to join the tarmac road. A steep hill took us back to Malham.

Reaching the tarmac road, near to Malham Tarn, we thought that the spectactular part of our walk was over, but we were mistaken. The disappearing river, at Water Sinks, was amazing, and it was even more amazing to read that this water did not re-appear at the cliff base, but at a spot near the weir that had been passed to the south of Malham, known as Aire Heads. The dry valley was impressive, with a lunar type landscape. Severe rock outcrops lined each side of the stony valley and the barrenness of the valley was emphasised by a dry stone wall running the full length of the gorge.

Traffic had eased considerably by the time we got back to Malham. Fewer people were on the bridges, and the residents of the cottages by the stream had picked up the chocolate wrappers and sweet papers that the uncaring visitors had left. The little cafe had a vacant table, so we had an indoor cup of tea while waiting for the bus to take us back to Gargrave.

When the bus came we found that it was the old-fashioned, courteous country service. We explained to the driver where we wanted to go, and asked to be dropped at the nearest bus stop. Kirkby Malham and Airton were recognised as the bus headed south, and the driver kept up a steady discourse on country affairs with his passengers. Then, ignoring bus stop signs, he pulled up at the campsite and bade us "Good-day and happy walking."

MALHAM TARN TO SILVERDALE ROAD

(An out and home walk of thirteen miles)

We reached the furthermost point of our previous walk in less than half an hour by car, and there was a parking place conveniently close to the Pennine Way sign (MR 98/897657) where the path crossed the road. The Tarn's grey surface was reflecting the unpromising, cloudy sky, but the forecast had said that rain was unlikely.

We followed the path over the wide grassy pasture and through a gateway to join the drive to Malham Tarn House. Our path led through a wooded area and behind the house which is now a field study centre. It then skirted round the northern banks of the Tarn. With rising ground on either side it headed north, over two stiles, and joined an unfenced road for a short stretch near Stangill Barn. The Pennine Way sign was on our left as we walked the few yards along this road, and it directed us up the entrance to Tennant Gill Farm. Passing round the farm we picked up the old mine track which headed west. There was a small stream to our right and our route crossed this after about half a mile, as the path turned north. After the stream we crossed an old stone wall and headed north to pick up a small cairn on a hillock, and then swung to a bearing averaging 35 degrees west of north, to skirt the summit of Fountains Fell. This was along old, indistinct mine paths, with occasional cairns to guide us. Our path passed close to old mine shafts and then dropped steeply towards the tarmac road ahead. About two hundred yards before the road we picked up a level grass track, running almost parallel to the road, and headed southwest towards Dale Head and the Silverdale Road.

Dull skies dampen the spirits, and this walk seemed uninspiring after the wonders of Malham Cove, and we tired quickly. We had anticipated some exciting bird life round the edges of the tarn, but everything seemed to have moved to the opposite bank, or flown to some sunny spot. The climb up and over Fountains Fell was hard on the legs, and we were never absolutely sure that we were on the right track, although these fears were groundless. This was an out and home walk, we had studied our maps and decided against a

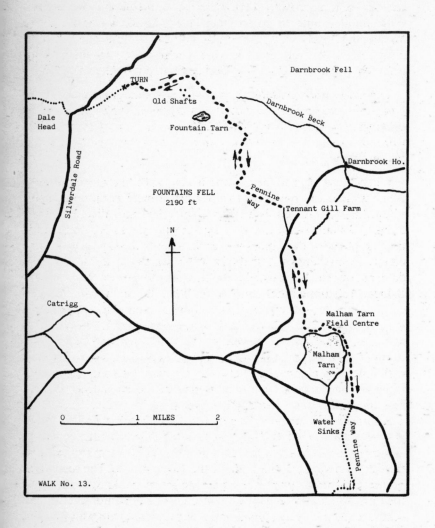

Darnbrook Fell

TURN

Old Shafts

Fountain Tarn

Darnbrook Beck

Dale
Head

Silverdale Road

Darnbrook Ho.

FOUNTAINS FELL
2190 ft

Pennine
Way

Tennant Gill Farm

N

Catrigg

Malham Tarn
Field Centre

Malham
Tarn

0   1   MILES   2

Water
Sinks

Pennine Way

WALK No. 13.

52

circular walk as it would have entailed six or seven miles of road walking, and that would have depressed us even further.

As we circumvented Fountains Fell there was a fantastic view of Penyghent, it looked sombre against the grey sky, but we were anxious for tomorrow to come when we would climb to its summit. With about a mile to go to Dale Head the skies became more threatening, heavy clouds swept in, and the summit of Penyghent disappeared. We retreated, leaving a marker; we would pick up from that point on the morrow, and climb that mountain.

The return walk to Malham Tarn was along the same paths as we had walked earlier in the day. It was easier because checking our bearings was unnecessary, and we knew that our path was right without constant reference to the map. The tarn was reached, and it had not rained.

When we got back to the caravan it was to normal "move routine", which we had now perfected to a fine art. A meal was prepared and eaten, kit was stowed away, dues were paid and the site owner thanked. Heading northwest on the A65 the sun broke through for the first time that day and as we reached Settle the sky cleared completely. From there we took the B6479 towards Horton-in-Ribblesdale, but our site book listed nothing nearer to Horton than Helwith Bridge. We stopped there only to find that the site was limited to a certain number of nights that it could open during the year. Whether this was to one of them we never found out. The welcome was so insincere that we moved on. We weren't worried by this. The camping area was a level patch, the size of a tennis court, covered with limestone chippings. The whole area seemed to be smothered in white dust from a huge quarry nearby. We moved on towards Horton, hoping to see something on the roadside.

Approaching Horton village there was a camp sign and we asked if a pitch was available. Their site was restricted to tents, and they couldn't take us, but they directed us to a friendly farm site, with no facilities, on the opposite bank of the River Ribble. The result was perfect for us. Our pitch was on a wide grassy bank, with a track to the farm and nowhere else on one side, and a beautiful river on the other. A steep railway embankment was covered with wild flowers, and the Settle to Carlisle train rumbled past occasionally. The water was at the farm, nearly half a mile away, and the toilet disposal was down a deep hole (with cover) in the farmyard. It was a heavenly spot and the tranquillity of the site far outweighed any of the inconveniences.

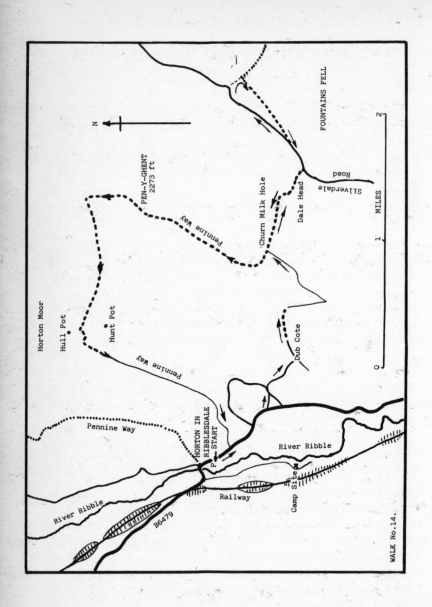

WALK No.14.

54

SILVERDALE ROAD TO HORTON-IN-RIBBLESDALE

(A circular walk of twelve miles)

The beautiful location, the bubbling River Ribble on our door-step, and bright blue skies overhead rapidly dispelled any gloom that lingered from our previous walk. From our site, near Crag Hill, Penyghent dominated the valley, its craggy summit beckoned and we looked forward to climbing it and having lunch at the top. We took the car into the village and turned south to find a convenient parking place on our right, and our walk started from there. (MR 98/726807).

We walked southwards on the main road, B6479, noticing the exit from the Pennine Way, which we would use on our return. We continued past the church and took the second tarmac road on our left, about a quarter of a mile from the start. This climbed gently and our chosen path was the second on the right, which headed for Dub Cote. There the lane forked and we took the track to the left, starting in a walled section, and then climbed east, on a path, to meet another cart track heading almost south. This took us to Long Lane, which was walled in places, and ran north east to Churn Milk Hole. The mass of Penyghent was to our left, and almost due east was our turning point of the previous walk. We turned right to the Silverdale road, and then left along the road for about a mile, to a small bridge. About two hundred yards, due south, up the bank, was our previous "surrender" point on the Pennine Way. We climbed to it, and then down the track to the road and Churn Milk Hole.

Our first visit to Churn Milk Hole was our stopping point for our morning tea. We looked back down the valley over the pleasant countryside that had been covered. The short walk on the B road had been quiet in idyllic surroundings, enjoyable with no traffic. The little countryside lanes to Dub Cote had passed between pleasant hedgerows, and the old barn there had been converted into a bunk house barn. We climbed quite steeply from there but it was so peaceful that the gradient wasn't noticed and Churn Milk Hole was soon reached, and surprisingly it was time for elevenses.

It seemed a pity that we could not turn immediately to Penyghent which was so close on our left, but our promise was to cover every foot of the Pennine Way, and ahead of us was about three miles of out and back walking, to compensate for the curtailment of our previous walk. An advantage was that it allowed us to stand back and view the mountain from the green lane on Fountains Fell. The lane was obviously an old mine road and offered comfortable walking, but ahead we could see the stiff rocky climb to the flat cap of Penyghent.

Having walked to our previous turning point on the Fountains Fell we headed towards the summit, climbed the stile with its acorn symbol, and then picked our way up the steep slope, over or around rock outcrops, to the broken down wall near the summit cairn. The track followed a wall north for about four hundred yards and then turned left down the steep eastern side of Penyghent. Following the track we passed through a gate, and then turning left, through another gate, and on to a wicket gate and stone hut. From that point to Horton-in-Ribblesdale there was a walled green lane descending steeply to the B6479, almost opposite our parked car.

As we scrambled and rested, scrambled and rested on the southern slopes of Penyghent, we could not avoid noticing the two youthful walkers who had rounded Fountains Fell. They were rapidly reducing the gap that separated us. Their urgency seemed obvious and we could readily imagine the suggestion that they would show the pair of slowcoaches in front how to climb. As we rested to regain our breath, they came round a rock outcrop and saw us face to face for the first time. They didn't need to speak, their faces showed their surprise at finding that they had caught up with a couple of oldies. The Pennine Way courtesy that we found everywhere, triumphed. They stopped and chatted, and the rest of the mountain was climbed together, at our pace.

There were beautiful views all around from this high point. The Silverdale Road wound its way to Halton Gill, and south of the road was Fountains Fell. To the west was Ingleborough, and north was Whernside. Down below was Horton, where only a slight breeze had stirred the leaves, but it had grown to half a gale on this mountain top. We looked for a sheltered spot to have our picnic, and left our two young companions on the summit. We found a cosy corner just below the strata of rocks, with a beautiful outlook.

The descent was easy and the path distinct. On reaching the walled section we made a slight detour to look at Hunt Pot and Hull Pot, but felt no desire to investigate the subterranean caves and passages. Our pleasure came from seeing birds and flowers, and wide open spaces. We strolled down the lane to Horton, and then back to our riverside camp, hoping to see a train loaded with rail enthusiasts and sightseers. As a train chugged past, once again, we said "Some day."

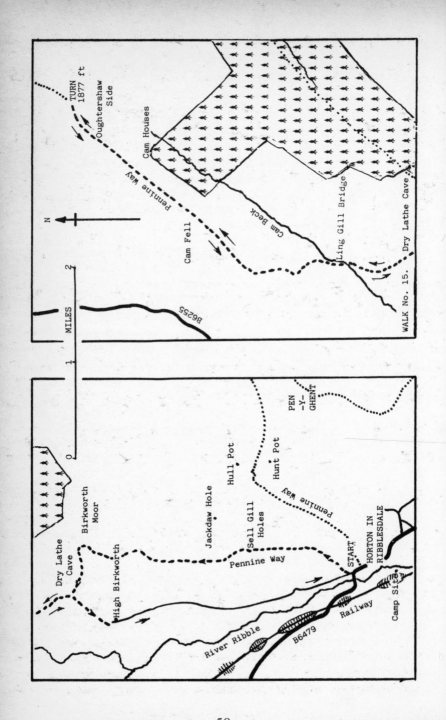

N

MILES
0   1   2

WALK No. 15. Dry Lathe Cave.

TURN 1877 ft
Oughtershaw Side

Pennine Way

Cam Houses

Cam Fell

Cam Beck

Ling Gill Bridge

B6255

PEN
-Y-
GHENT

Dry Lathe Cave

Birkworth Moor

High Birkworth

Jackdaw Hole

Hull Pot

Hunt Pot

Sell Gill Holes

Pennine Way

Pennine Way

START

HORTON IN
RIBBLESDALE

River Ribble

B6479

Railway

Camp Site

HORTON-IN-RIBBLESDALE TO CAM HOUSES

(A partly circular walk of sixteen miles)

With the caravan parked in such an idyllic setting there was a tendency to just sit and listen to nature, but this Pennine Way bug bites deeply. Once the walk is started there is a peculiar driving force that is forever urging forward.

Heading north from MR 98/726807 up an opening by the side of the village pub we were soon strolling up an attractive, walled green lane to Sell Gill Holes. There the walled section ended, but a distinct path continued northwards for almost two miles to Birkwith Moor. The path then turned west to Old Ing and, being joined by a track from the southwest, turned to the north once more and headed for Cam Beck and Ling Gill Bridge. Crossing the bridge we still headed in a generally northerly direction, to reach the cairn at Cam End, and there joined the old Roman road, running northeast. We followed this, passing Cam Houses, below on our right, and for a short way walked on an unfenced tarmac road. On reaching the high point, where the road turned to the east, and the Pennine Way went northeast, we decided that there was a suitable turning point.

A little over a mile of the lane from Horton had been covered when we saw our first large pothole. Still Gill Hole had a protective fence but we peered into this cavity that stretched under our feet, and marvelled, but were not tempted to venture underground. The tree fringed Jackdaw Hole was on our left, and there were several other potholes to our right; it seemed to be a cavers' paradise. The hillside was vastly different to the hills further south where everything had appeared grey, with dark brown patches of peat and lying water. Here the close cropped grass was green, and the hillsides were covered with irregular small hollows. Walking up the gently climbing well-defined track was much easier than scrambling through peat bogs. After passing the lonely farmstead at Old Ing, we dropped gently to the stream that passed under Ling Gill Bridge and looked down the tree lined ravine. This was a natural spot for a cup of tea so we sat on the bridge wall. An inscription on the bridge told us that the whole of the West Riding paid for its construction in

1765; the bridge had outlived the West Riding. We enjoyed the tranquility of the spot.

This was a spot that tempted one to loiter. Long hours could have been spent exploring this rock strewn gorge. The piles of boulders and the near vertical rock walls suggested that in years past this had been a huge cave. Fighting the temptation to linger we moved on, there was at least another four miles to our turning point, perhaps someday we would come back to Ling Gill and explore.

We soon reached Cam End, where we joined the old Roman Road. Beautiful open views surrounded us, fresh breezes cooled us and bright sunshine cheered us as we strolled along to our turning point. It was a fabulous lookout spot. Looking down Snaizeholme Beck we saw a trickle of water grow to a gleaming stream. Whernside and Ingleborough were still dominant and Penyghent was just visible. A nearby seat provided a sophisticated picnic spot with only sheep for company.

The walk back was a gentle downhill stroll, following the same route past Ling Gill Bridge to where the path turned east at Old Ing. We went straight ahead, on a bearing a little to the west of south, to strike a narrow tarmac road at High Birkworth. We followed this traffic free road downhill to Horton and the car to complete a fairly long but relatively easy walk.

It was a pleasant stroll back to the car as we gradually lost height. Once again we resisted the temptation to wander from our planned route and explore Ling Gill, we could have spent an hour or more in that beautiful wooded valley but we had a caravan move scheduled following this walk. Near Old Ing we looked west and could see the amazing delicacy of the Ribblehead viaduct, and as we followed the tarmac road there were some fine views of the Ribble valley. When we reached the end of the lane we looked at our map, we had joined the B6479 and the map said New Inn, but we could only find the Crown, but what's in a name to a thirsty walker?

The evening move was an easy, straight-forward operation. Heading north on the B6479 we followed the Ribble Valley and the famous railway line to the T junction with the B6255, which follows the course of another old Roman road. Here the River Ribble had been downgraded to Gayle Beck, and the railway left the road to bury itself in a tunnel prior to crossing the majestic Ribblehead viaduct.

Turning right at the T junction we passed over the watershed at Gayle Moor, and followed the beck down to Widdale, towards Hawes. Our small chosen site, Honeycott, was on the left of the road, just before entering Hawes.

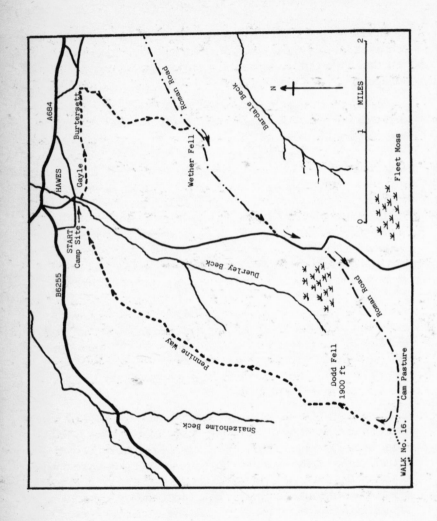

WALK No. 16.

CAM HOUSES TO GAYLE

(A circular walk of fifteen miles)

The Honeycott site, on which we were parked, was almost opposite a road through to Gayle, which was less than a mile away, so we left the car with the caravan and strode out for this pretty dale village.

The minor road running almost due south from the B6255 at MR 98/864896 turned to the left after about a quarter of a mile and ran east into the village of Gayle. Our route turned left and then right, crossing the river and climbing out of the village. Here a small lane led to the left and then forked and we took the left fork, and followed vague field paths in an easterly direction to pick up a walled track into Buttersett. Before reaching the tarmac we turned right and made a double bend, and then climbed steadily in a southwest direction for a mile. We left this fairly distinct track and headed for the old Roman road, about three hundred yards ahead, taking a path to the east of the high ground (Wether Fell). We turned right on the old road, still heading more or less southwest. After about one and a half miles the tarmac road that climbed steeply from Gayle to Langstrothdale was reached. This was followed uphill to the sharp bend to the left and our track went straight ahead on the old Roman road. This took us round the southern slopes of Dodd Fell, swinging round to the west or even slightly north of west. We met the Pennine Way at Kidhow Gate, our former turning point, at the head of Snaizeholme Beck.

The village of Gayle was a real treat, and we marked it down for a later, more leisurely visit. A rushing stream thrust its way under a stone bridge and some really old buildings lined the quiet road. The actual Pennine Way skirts the village proper, but we passed through it and enjoyed its rural charm. There was a building contractor's store in an old house bearing the date 1669, and we wondered what would remain of more recent properties in over 300 years' time. From the field path beyond Gayle there was a fantastic view of the wide Wensleydale valley, with roads on each side of the meandering River Ure. We perspired freely as we climbed towards Wether Fell and were pleased to strike the relatively easy gradients chosen by the Romans for their road. Reaching the tarmac there were more wonderful views when looking towards Gayle, with Duerby Beck in the valley bottom. Skirting around Dodd Fell we could see the road twisting its way to Upper Wharfedale and Buckden. The view, and a convenient grassy bank, tempted us and we had our picnic in idyllic surroundings before heading for our Pennine Way joining point.

The Way ran northeast along the steep slope of Dodd Fell, on a well defined path, practically maintaining the same height throughout. The cairn at Ten End was a positive landmark. From there our footpath veered slightly to the right, while the main track headed north to join the B road. Our path dropped steeply to join a farm track at Gaudy House Farm, and then developed into a tarmac road heading towards Gayle. This led to the minor tarmac road on which we had started our walk and we then turned left to return to our caravan.

The breeze had hardly been noticed as we had climbed down from Gayle but at Kidhow Gate it had grown to a very pronounced wind. It swept up the valley, being funnelled by the steep slopes of Snaizeholme and Dodd Fell, but as we walked in a northerly direction the stone wall on our left broke the force of the wind. As we stepped clear of the wall, or passed a wide gap, the force of the wind would carry us several feet up the slope. Part of this path to Ten End was hard paved track that was easy to follow and pleasant underfoot. From there the track gave us a wonderful view of Wensleydale and of the land ahead. Almost due north was Great Shunner Fell, our next hurdle, with its gently rounded summit, and to its right the road leading over Buttertubs Pass. Tomorrow we would view them from a different angle.

This walk had provided some of the most spectacular and attractive views so far on the Pennine Way. Our preference for wide open spaces had been satisfied and on all sides we had glorious backdrops of mountainous and deep green valleys.

WALK 17
GAYLE TO THWAITE

(A one way walk of eleven miles)

Once again we had been promised one-way transport and we were thankful. The original plan was to walk from Gayle to the summit of Great Shunner Fell, and then return by a circular route to Hawes. The next day the process would be repeated from Thwaite, making two twelve mile walks and two climbs up the mountain. The offer of transport meant that the journey could be made in one trip, so saving at least twelve miles and, more important for "not so young" legs, a climb of 2340 feet.

We started from the site, Honeycott, and took the same minor road as the previous day to reach the Pennine Way to pass through Gayle. This route didn't cross the bridge over Duerby Beck but turned alongside it towards Hawes. After a couple of hundred yards a path on our right was joined. A flagged path led towards the church and took us to the shopping centre of Hawes. We turned right on this loop road and at the end, at the car park, crossed the A684 on to the minor road to Hardraw. A two arch bridge spans the River Ure and shortly afterwards a stile on the left leads to a paved path across a field, and eventually to a group of houses that constitute Hardraw. A slight detour through the Green Dragon was made to Hardraw Force. We left at the west end of the hamlet and turned right on a walled track that climbed steeply towards Great Shunner Fell. The walled path ended at a gate leading to the moorland, but the path was still distinct, and here and there cairns had been built making navigation easy. The next natural landmark was the Jingle-mea Crag on our left and then a further cairn, Crag End beacon, and a mile or so further on the summit of the mountain.

Leaving the summit we headed northeast towards another cairn which was not as striking as Crag End. About a mile past this smaller cairn, continuing in the same direction, the Pennine Way turned southeast to pick up an old track that dropped quite steeply to meet the B6270 just north of Thwaite. We turned into Thwaite, on the tarmac road, found a seat and waited for our transport.

When planning these walks this had seemed a little frightening. Two thousand three hundred and forty feet seemed to be a long way up, the highest so far on the Pennine Way. But the climb had

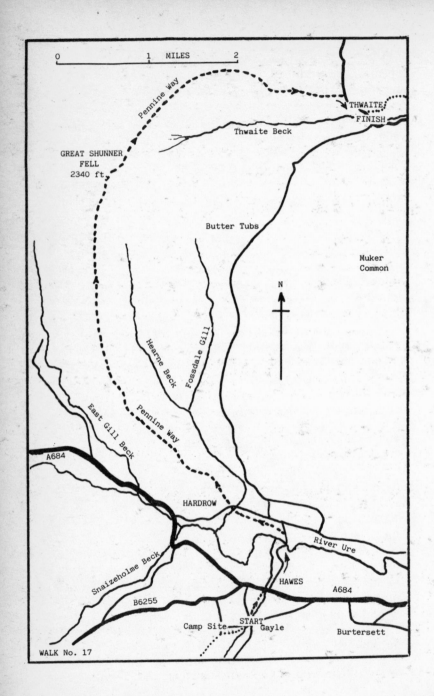

0   1   MILES   2

Pennine Way

GREAT SHUNNER
FELL
2340 ft.

Thwaite Beck

THWAITE
FINISH

Butter Tubs

Muker
Common

N

Hearne Beck

Fossdale Gill

East Gill Beck

Pennine Way

A684

HARDROW

River Ure

Snaizeholme Beck

HAWES

A684

B6255

Camp Site   START   Gayle

Burtersett

WALK No. 17

66

been relatively gentle. We hadn't hurried, our saunter through the narrow streets of Hawes allowed us to look at walking gear in one of the shop windows, and we watched the water of Duerby Beck appear in the town centre and then splash its way underground. The stop at Hardraw Force is almost obligatory, unless one is a Pennine Way walker who hopes to cover the entire route in ten days or less. The river wasn't in spate, but a transparent white ribbon of water still made its plunge of about a hundred feet—it wasn't Niagara but it was ours!

The climb was constant but reasonably gentle from the road at Hardraw to the summit. Younger walkers caught up with us, chatted and then with cheery goodbyes surged ahead. Here and there were old coal pits, and other scars left by man that nature was trying to cover. The visibility was perfect and we were entranced with the wonderful views. Across the valley was the road climbing up to the viewpoint at the Buttertubs, and beyond was Abbotside Common and wild Oxnop Moor, where we had previously walked, never dreaming that we would ever be courageous enough to climb Great Shunner Fell and walk the full Pennine Way.

The green grass disappeared on reaching the summit and we were on a plateau of dry dark peat. Thankfully the weather was fine and our track was dry, but several mining depressions we had passed were full of water. It was easy to appreciate that this friendly mountain could be a very hostile place in bad weather and zero visibility. The grey walled cottages of Thwaite and Muker nestled in the valley, and that ubiquitous ribbon of tarmac wound its way through the unspoiled green fields of Swaledale.

The peat path gave way to an old cart track, with gorse and bramble spreading from the tumbling hedges. In places the adjacent stream also joined the track and we splashed through tiny puddles of crystal clear water. At the end of the lane was a Pennine Way sign and we followed its direction into the village of Thwaite. An ice cream, a seat in the sun and a chat to fellow walkers. It was there that we met a clergyman in mufti who expressed the opinion that nowhere, either in the church or in everyday life had he met with as much good fellowship as he had encountered along the Pennine Way. We couldn't agree more!

With happy memories of our day's walk to mull over we waited for our daughter to arrive with transport to take us back over the Buttertubs to our caravan. The following day we went back home.

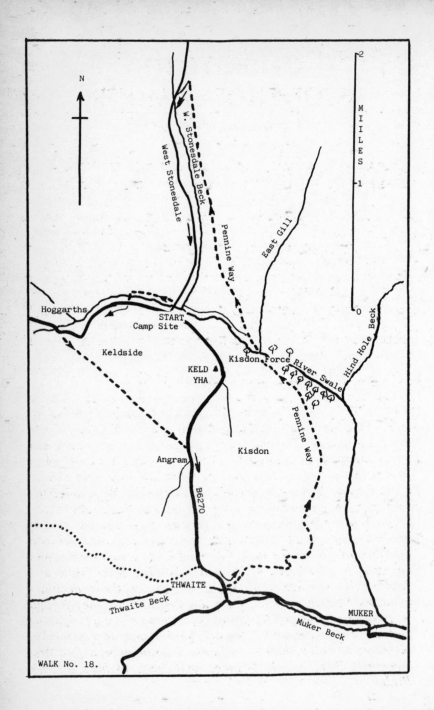

WALK No. 18.

68

WALK 18
THWAITE TO STONEHOUSE MOOR
(A circular walk of eleven miles)

Having returned home from Thwaite at the end of June, and despite having had a holiday walking over Dartmoor in July, we were still very anxious to get back to our Pennine Way adventure. In mid-August we managed it. The caravan was hitched to the car and we headed up the M1 and A1 and then west to Keld in Swaledale. This remote cluster of houses hardly warrants the title of village, it has a Youth Hostel and a chapel, but no pub or shop. It is a delightful spot and the YHA chose wisely. We went beyond the village and parked at a small site immediately before the Tan Hill turn-off. Once again the site was on a river bank, with waterfalls both up and down stream. The water level was rather low so the falls were not spectacular, but the entire area had a great deal of charm. At that time it seemed to have a special attraction for midges, minute flying insects with an insatiable desire for human blood.

The walk started from the campsite at Park Bridge (MR 92/886015). We crossed the bridge and took a footpath on the north bank of the River Swale, recrossing the river after about half a mile to join the road (B6270) and headed west. In about three quarters of a mile the road bent sharply to cross the river but our route was a faint path that led off in a southeast direction over Keld Side to rejoin the road midway between Keld and Thwaite. We followed the road into Thwaite and wended our way between the houses to pick up the Pennine Way footpath sign, heading firstly east, but turning northeast through small paddocks, with stone walls, and across a field towards a barn. The track led round Kisdon, with several stiles en route, to pass below a limestone cliff. The River Swale and Kisdon Force were in a deep gorge to our right, and the small cluster of houses, Keld, to our left. A footbridge took us across the river and we passed a sign saying "Coast to Coast Footpath". At a fork in the path we chose to head north towards Tan Hill and, after two miles, picked up a small path on our left, heading southwest, to join West Stonesdale Road, which, heading south, took us back to Park Bridge.

From the start this walk provided beautiful scenery. Strolling up the northern river bank we passed a series of step-like waterfalls, with white water interspersed with still pools. A couple of anglers were flicking their lines over the surface of the water, but did not appear to get any response from the fish. Behind us, as we climbed over Keld Side was Whitsundale and the beck flowing down from Ravenseat. On our left was the valley that carried the road to Tan Hill, and snuggling in the valley our white caravan in virtual isolation. The surrounds of wild hills and twisting valleys, tumbling waterfalls and blue skies were the lure that had drawn us back. As we approached the tarmac road Kisdon Hill seemed to dominate the view and our thoughts, but this was one hill that we would circumnavigate rather than climb. This strange conical hill stood like a giant pimple between two deep valleys, the one to the east carrying the River Swale and the one to the west the public highway.

The cluster of grey buildings at the foot of the hill was Thwaite, famous as the birthplace of two naturalist brothers Richard and Cherry Kearton. The village was active, young walkers of both sexes, obviously from the Youth Hostel at Keld were besieging the small souvenir shop, and consuming ice cream. We had our cup of tea and searched around to find the Pennine Way track through a network of stone walls. After crossing a field we picked our way gingerly, through a stone-walled section that was knee deep in mud. This wasn't the clean, sterile peat that we had encountered on our earlier walks, but wet earth, with certain animal additions that had been kneaded to a semi-fluid state by the feet of scores of cattle. Stiles seemed to abound in this area, many of them of the squeezer variety, where it was difficult to let one boot pass the other in the narrow gap at the base.

From this path, skirting Kisdon, we could look down Swaledale. We tried to count the number of stone barns that were dotted around the spread of green fields, but each count gave a different answer. The proliferation of these solid stone structures indicated that the area suffered severe winters or that all the farmers were very kindly animal loving souls.

As we passed the limestone cliffs and entered a wooden area the trees screened the river from view but allowed the tantalising sound of falling water to tempt us. Eventually curiosity won and we left the official Pennine Way path and descended a steep path to see Kisdon Force. Even with the river at a reduced flow it was well worthwhile. A beautiful, two-tier waterfall, not of spectacular

70

height, but a mass of rushing white water against a backdrop of green foliage, with flat shelves of limestone forming parapets on each side of the river. It was easy to imagine the splendour of this section of river when it was in full spate. Even with this reduced flow one could sense the power of that white water as it dashed over the stepped rocks. It contrasted vividly with the still pools and the bracken covered slopes that stretched upwards towards Stonesdale.

We returned to our planned path and shortly dropped down to the river once more, to cross a wooden footbridge near to another smaller waterfall, on East Gill Beck. Here again there was beauty. There was less water than on Kisdon, but a higher, more direct fall compensated for this. Small ferns had rooted into the fissures of the rocks had flourished in the constant spray. Our path climbed steeply for a short stretch after the bridge and passed the sign "Coast to Coast Walk". This tempted us to say "We must try that sometime," but we feel that the path must pass through a great deal of arable, agricultural land, and our favourite terrain is the wide open moorland.

As the path levelled we could look back over West Stonesdale on the opposite side of the valley and the road that was to take us back to Park Bridge, where we could see our caravan, now joined by two small tents. We would have company for the evening.

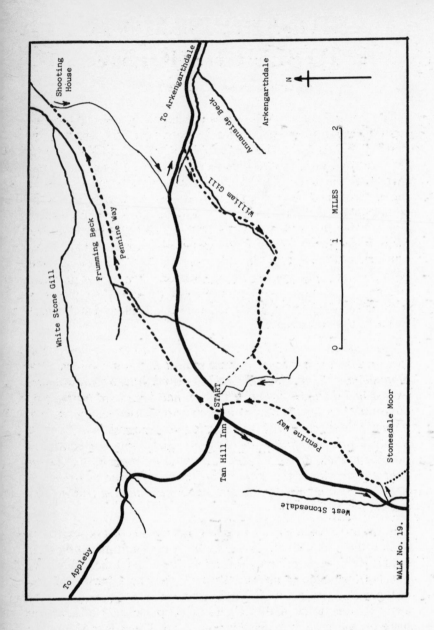

STONEHOUSE MOOR
TO SLEIGHTHOLME

(A circular walk of thirteen miles)

The true start of this walk was only a couple of miles up the road from our campsite at Park Bridge but we could forsee no suitable parking area on that relatively narrow road. So we took the car up the road to Tan Hill, where there was ample parking, and left it there. Our planned route was a figure of eight walk with a circuit to the south of Tan Hill being followed by one to the north. This is the site of an isolated, mountain top inn, the highest public house in England, which was featured in a certain double glazing advertisement. It is a barren, lonely spot with no other apparent habitation, but it was built to cater for the miners in this area in days long gone. Now it relies on the tourist as even the crude shelters that provided sleeping accommodation for the miners, close to their places of work, seem to have crumbled and have been swallowed and hidden by the heather and gorse.

From the car park at Tan Hill (MR 91/896067) at the junction of two unclassified roads we headed almost due south on the West Stonesdale road, up which we had just driven. After about two miles we reached the track on our left which had been used on our previous walk. This path doubled back in a northeast direction, near to a small bridge where the beck passed under the road. In a couple of hundred yards we joined the Pennine Way route and continued northeast for a mile or so, then the path turned more north, passing near a quarry and some old mine workings. The tarmac road was struck about a hundred yards east of the road junction and we were back at the car park.

It was our aversion to walking on tarmac roads that prompted us to start the walk with this short southerly circuit. It meant that our hard surface walk was down hill and was over and done with before our morning break. It also saved carrying any pack for this section of the walk. Despite our dislike of road walking the area was very attractive, the traffic, mid-week, was very sparse and we were soon back on the moorland. Walking back up Stonesdale Moore we could see the road and so felt ourselves to be part of civilisation without becoming too involved. We had our tea by the car and then set off with our pack, with waterproofs, flasks and food.

From Tan Hill we joined the Pennine Way path, heading northeast over Sleightholme Moore and soon picked up a small stream that led us to Frumming Beck. At the confluence of the tributaries we crossed the stream but still kept close to the bank with the meandering stream on our left. Shortly after passing a building (the OS map marks it as a shooting house) the path developed into a distinct cart track, and joined a wide farm road coming in from the south. We turned and joined this farm road and headed south, veering southwest to join the tarmac road from Reeth to Tan Hill.

Shortly after leaving the dusty car park we found that we were picking our way over dry ground with tufts of coarse grass and wet spongy patches with moss covered pools to either side. As the stream developed the ground became better drained, less care was needed and the walking became very pleasant. Gorse, heather and rough furze surrounded close cropped grassy areas. The usual meadow pipits and winchats bobbed about, and wagtails hunted insects near the water's edge. In dry patches of bare peaty earth we found small pieces of coal that reminded us that in the past this was a coal producing area. Day holes were worked by under-paid miners and the population was increased by the pedlars, tinkers and camp followers anxious to get a share of the miners' meagre wages.

The shooting house was an indication of a less strenuous occupation, and a more affluent standard of living followed by the landed gentry. To prove the point a few red grouse broke cover and noisily skimmed over the bushes as we approached. The pleasant, broad unfenced farm track that headed back to the tarmac road made an ideal picnic spot. We sat and idly stared over a peaceful, deserted landscape, it was a relaxation that came very easily and is quite addictive.

When we had reached the tarmac road we turned left, towards Reeth, for about half a mile, until a stream came in from our right and ran alongside the road. There our route turned upstream in a southerly direction, up William Gill for about a mile and a half, to reach some old mine workings. We looked for the footpath that was marked on the map, to lead us back to Tan Hill. We found a track leading in the right direction and in about a mile located an old mine road that twisted from west to north but brought us back to the road within sight of Tan Hill.

This seemed to be a day for walking beside streams, and we enjoyed the sound of running water, the birds, dragonflies and other insects that it attracted, but William Gill did not have the charm of Frumming Beck. There seemed to be more signs of man's interference with nature, and, in places, we could sense that this was a mine stream. The surrounds tended to be more confining and once away from the stream we stumbled through fairly dense gorse, brambles and heather, and over some very uneven ground. It was a relief to hit the old mine road and we were content to follow that rather than search further for the planned footpath.

When we emerge from a fairly isolated and deserted stretch of moorland there is always a glow of satisfaction to see the car just where we had left it several hours earlier. In many cases there are no other vehicles in sight but at Tan Hill it was different and several cars were parked in the car park and people were sitting around picnicking. We drove back to our caravan and had our meal on the banks of the River Swale.

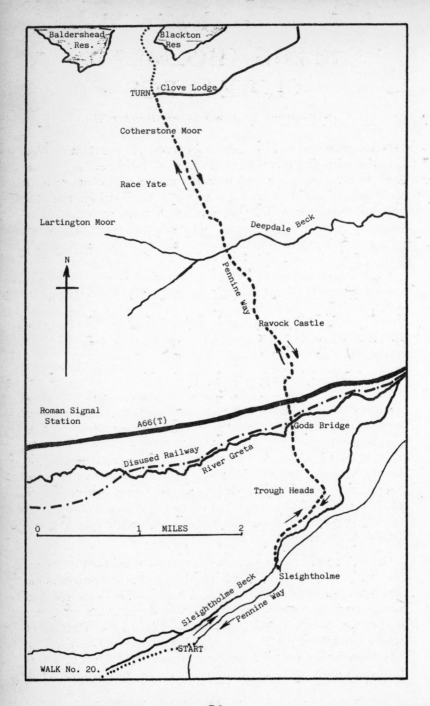

Baldershead
Res.

Blackton
Res.

TURN Clove Lodge

Cotherstone Moor

Race Yate

Lartington Moor

Deepdale Beck

N

Pennine Way

Ravock Castle

Roman Signal
Station

A66(T)

Gods Bridge

Disused Railway

River Greta

Trough Heads

0   1   MILES   2

Sleightholme

Sleightholme Beck

Pennine Way

START

WALK No. 20.

76

SLEIGHTHOLME TO CLOVE LODGE

(An out and home walk of fourteen miles)

We thought long and hard about this stretch of the Pennine Way. Circular walks are preferable but there are some sections of this long distance footpath that do not lend themselves to such an arrangement, and this was one such walk. Any variation from the out and home pattern was going to lengthen the walk quite considerably, although there is an alternative Pennine Way route through Bowes for any who are prepared to make one very long walk or two short walks.

The decision was made. We drove from Park Bridge to Tan Hill and turned right on the Reeth road. After about two miles we picked up the tarmac farm road leading to Sleightholme and, in just over a mile, near the shooting house, we joined the Pennine Way. There was no problem parking there, acres of wide open moorland and meandering Sleightholme Beck.

Leaving the car near the junction (MR 91/940092) our route was down a gently falling metalled lane in a northeasterly direction, running parallel to the beck. We passed through a gate and between farm buildings at Sleightholme Farm and continued on the metalled road until we reached a gate on the left, with a Pennine Way sign pointing towards the beck. A footbridge took us over the stream, and we climbed up a steep bank to pick up a path along the top of the escarpment. Trough Head farmhouse was soon reached (light refreshments available), and a further sign indicated a turn slightly west of north and a reasonably distinct path was followed to God's Bridge, the old railway track and the A66 crossing.

This proved to be a pleasant start to our walk and not too strenuous. The tranquil greenery of the river valley at Sleightholme contrasted sharply with the dampish moorland that we had encountered upstream on the previous walk, and with the dense heather and gorse, that we skirted around on the moorland, after leaving Trough Heads. But the valley of the River Greta was an even more idyllic contrast. Here we crossed God's Bridge where the rock forms a natural span over the river. The river level was low and it was possible for me to crouch beside the stream and take a photograph of my wife through this natural bridge. Books tell us of vast caves and tunnels that extend for thousands of feet under or through this limestone bed. We are prepared to take the author's word for it and have no desire to explore.

After crossing the bridge we climbed to the old railway track and then up again to the busy A66 with its steady stream of vehicles, either hurtling madly towards Bowes, or climbing laboriously towards the summit, and points west. The tang of gorse and heather was replaced by the fumes of diesel and we hurried on.

A sign to a well-trodden path, with some cairns led us from the A66 to Ravock Castle. From there, in open country with few special features we kept on a rough bearing of 335 degrees and descended into the shallow valley of Deepdale Beck. Then heading for a slight depression in the skyline we spotted the old stone of Race Yate, on the high point ahead. Reaching the stone we were then able to view the Balderstone valley with its reservoirs, and the small clump of trees near Clove Lodge. That was our target and turning point.

Ravock Castle was a disappointment, with a name such as that we expected something more impressive than the few remains of a shepherd's shelter. The site would have afforded a good place for a castle, it had a dominating position over the valley, but there seemed little to protect except miles and miles of desolation. Even the rough scrub and furze seemed to be struggling to survive, and the depressions in the baked soil were filled with smooth, crack-crazed mud. We were thankful that it wasn't wet, and that we were dusty rather than mud-caked. Even Deepdale Beck was struggling for existence, and a footbridge seemed an unnecessary luxury to cross such an insignificant drop of water. The walking was easy under these conditions and we certainly left no footprints.

As we crested the hill the gleaming waters of the reservoirs in Balderdale were a welcome sight, and the clump of trees round Clove Lodge made an attractive aiming point. With all this open country it was difficult to accept that we were having to retrace our steps back to Sleightholme. The starting point of our walk was almost due south from Clove Lodge, and we had arrived by making a slightly circuitous route to the east, but there were no marked footpaths across Lartington High Moor and Bowes Moor.

Retracing our outward journey we headed for the boundary stone at Race Yate, then down to the footbridge over Deepdale Beck and on to Ravock Castle. Another downhill stretch took us across the A66 to God's Bridge and then we climbed over Wytham Moor on the same distinct footpath to Trough Heads on the steep escarpment overlooking Sleightholme Beck.

Meals and refreshments had been taken en route in our usual picnicking fashion, but the sign for refreshments at Trough Heads was tempting. The day was hot, and we had passed the ten mile mark, so we decided we would pick up a couple of cans of lemonade and sit on the valley edge, with a fabulous view of Sleightholme Beck, and drink it. But no! We could not buy cans to take out, we could consume it on the premises, but the proprietor was not going to give anyone the opportunity to litter the moors with empty "pop" cans. Having seen, and condemned such inconsiderate litter, we wholeheartedly agreed with him. I find it impossible to understand why a walker, or anyone else, can find room and energy to carry a full can of drink to a distant beauty spot, but hasn't the room, energy or consideration for others, to carry a light, empty can away. We certainly did not want to sit inside to drink, but agreed to transfer the drinks into our empty flasks, deposit the cans in his bin, and drink our lemonade wherever we wished.

From Trough Heads our homeward path was completely straightforward. Once we had descended to the beck and crossed the bridge to the tarmac farm road, we stayed on this well-maintained road to the car.

Another stretch of the Pennine Way was completed and another move was called for. Our destination was Middleton-in-Teesdale and there was no easy direct route. After our evening meal we left Keld and headed up the road to Tan Hill and turned left on to the unfenced moorland road. It was not an ideal caravan road but there appeared to be no alternative. By bearing right on these minor roads I emerged on to the A66 near Maiden Castle, and we headed westwards for Brough. Picking up the B6276, just before entering Brough, we followed it through to Middleton-in-Teesdale.

Our chosen site was a farm, by the river, at the east end of the village, where we have stayed on previous visits to the area. Leaving the village the road bears to the left but we headed straight on and passed by some garages to a lane behind a row of houses. This narrow lane, with few passing places leads to Leckworth Farm (MR 91/659203). The site is a peaceful field by the River Tees, with no facilities other than a water tap, but we like it.

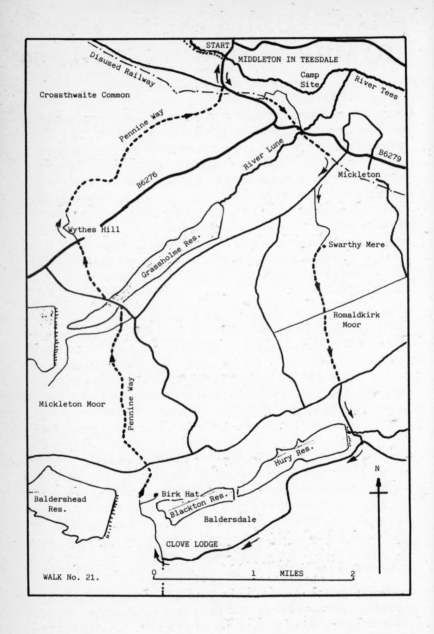

START
MIDDLETON IN TEESDALE
Camp Site
River Tees
B6279
Mickleton
Disused Railway
Crossthwaite Common
Pennine Way
B6276
River Lune
Wythes Hill
Grassholme Res.
Swarthy Mere
Romaldkirk Moor
Pennine Way
Mickleton Moor
Hury Res.
N
Baldershead Res.
Birk Hat
Blackton Res.
Baldersdale
CLOVE LODGE

WALK No. 21.

0   1   MILES   2

WALK 21
CLOVE LODGE, BALDERSDALE
TO MIDDLETON-IN-TEESDALE

(A circular walk of thirteen miles)

Leckworth Farm, in Middleton, is one of the few campsites that we have used more than once. Situated on the river bank, and well away from the road it is always peaceful. There is a good water supply and a toilet disposal point near to the farm. The village, which has an interesting connection with the old lead mining industry, is close at hand for supplies and petrol. On this occasion it had the added advantage of being only about a mile from the Pennine Way.

Knowing the site we settled in quickly, and in the morning, being familiar with the shops, had a quick shopping trip round the village, and we were able to leave our car parked in the main street for the rest of the day.

Starting our walk from the main street we turned south to cross the River Tees on the B6277. Shortly after the bridge there was a Pennine Way sign on our right, but that was for the next walk, the track for this walk was to the left, close to the river, and cutting off a bend in the road. Using vague footpaths and the old railway track we reached Mickleton. Near the start of the village we took a narrow road to our right, which had a caravan site sign post, and followed this for about half a mile, crossing over the old railway line. A farm track on our left led us to Swarthy Mere and we continued on a footpath across fields, heading practically due south. After crossing another farm road, a small clump of trees was passed to our left and a minor road was reached. A narrow road opposite dropped steeply to cross near the dam head of Hury Reservoir, we crossed and kept left to follow the southern bank as far as Willoughby Hall. The Ordnance Survey map shows footpaths through the meadows along the banks of the reservoirs, but we chose to follow the quiet, unfenced tarmac road for almost two miles to Clove Lodge.

We struggled a bit in the early stages of this walk, when we searched for the footpaths after crossing the Tees Bridge. It tended to make us frustrated as the rights of way were very indistinct and we always try not to trespass. If it was to be repeated we would probably use the road, at least for some of the walk to Mickleton. The old railway line could make a very attractive walk, but, in places, local farmers had used it for a cattle or a chicken run, etc. Gates and fences had been strung across the track, and, as is common with many farmers, the gates were difficult to open or were tied with unbreakable polypropylene.

The road and track after Mickleton took us over Romaldkirk Moor, and the peaceful open country compensated for the earlier frustration. The still waters of Hury Reservoir, and its neighbour, Blackton, spelled out tranquillity, but this was summertime. We knew that in winter this area can be cut off from the outside world for weeks at a time, that water supplies on the farms can be frozen, and that the ice on the reservoirs has to be broken to draw water to feed both the farmers and their stock. The meadows that skirted the reservoirs had animals grazing, and the paths across were not very apparent, and the quiet road and a stretch of easy walking was the choice. The rising moorland to the south of our road, Cotherstone Moor, looked grim and deserted, but we could spot the path down which we had come on our previous walk. The pleasant environs of Clove Lodge made a very satisfactory picnic spot.

Leaving Clove Lodge we joined the Pennine Way heading north. A road led down to Blackton Bridge, where captive streams have replaced the River Balder. Over the bridge we passed through water-works property, and then by lane to Birk Hat, and left to High Birk Hat Farm. A track climbed to the metalled road and almost opposite a faint path led over rough pasture up hill. After about a mile and half of farmland the path crossed over the head of Grassholme Reservoir in Lunedale. Once over Grassholme Bridge there was a further climb up to the B6276 and then up an old farm lane to Wythes Hill. The official path from this point was rather vague but we kept on minor tracks that ran to the northeast, and kept the distinctive clump of trees at Kilcarron on our right. Once the village of Middleton, and the Tees valley was visible we headed directly for the river crossing, and descended to join the Holwich road near the junction with the main Teesdale road. Half a mile ahead was the main street to the right, and the car.

This country of reservoirs has a distinct charm in bright, sunny weather. The waters glistened, swallows and house martins skimmed the surface but, despite the beauty we could not help lamenting the loss of our free running rivers, with small secluded pools, overhanging trees and miniature waterfalls. Concrete, man-made paths encroach on the rural splendour but as we passed over the bridge and climbed to High Birk Hat, farm tracks and wooded slopes re-asserted themselves. A short stretch of semi-wild scrubland, before dropping into Lunedale was countered by green pasture and fields in the valley, but the outstanding feature of the walk was the isolation. As we crested the hill and looked into Teesdale the isolation vanished. This had been a favourite of ours for years, and we paused near the trig point on Harter Fell (not to be confused with other Harter Fells) and picked out our much-loved landmarks. We could see the wide sweep of the river as the dale widened beyond Middleton, and our caravan shone white on a green sward, with a backcloth of trees, close to the river bank.

Across the river we could see Hudeshope Beck, flowing in from the north, and we recalled the old mineworkings that we had seen up there on previous walks. It was those mine workings that established Middleton as a community and an important market town in years past. Further upstream on the River Tees we could see Newbiggin and, behind it, Hardberry Hill, but it wasn't necessary to have names, or even memories, to enjoy the beauty of the wild, captivating valley. We'd been here before, we knew that we would come again. We looked up the dale and envisaged the next walk.

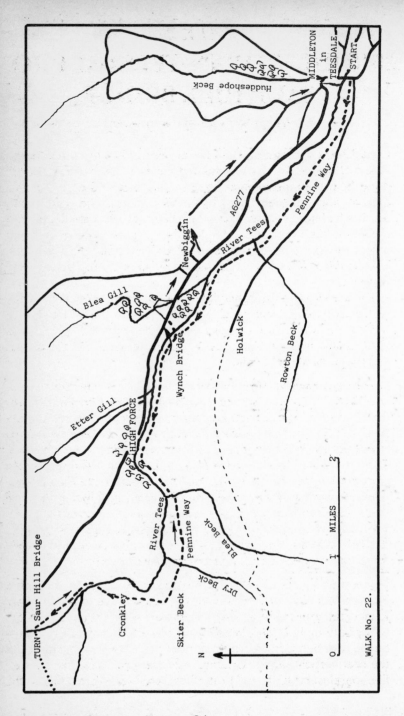

START

MIDDLETON in TEESDALE

Huddeshope Beck

Pennine Way

A6277

River Tees

Newbiggin

Blea Gill

Holwick

Rowton Beck

Wynch Bridge

Etter Gill

HIGH FORCE

River Tees

Pennine Way

Blea Beck

Dry Beck

Saur Hill Bridge

TURN

Cronkley

Skier Beck

N

0   1   2

MILES

WALK No. 22.

84

MIDDLETON-IN-TEESDALE TO SAUR HILL BRIDGE

(A circular walk of sixteen miles)

At 9.30 in the morning Middleton was not bustling with energy. A few of the locals were around, but the early starters had already done their shopping and had left the main street, and were probably hard at work on their farms or in their homes. The visitors and tourists had not yet arrived and Middleton was just a quiet market town on a non-market day. We left the car in the village to save a mile at the start and finish of the walk, and, as on our previous walk, we started by crossing the attractive single span bridge over the River Tees.

The mart was on the right of the road but it too was devoid of any real activity. The pens were all empty and a solitary figure in wellingtons was leisurely hosing down. The Pennine Way sign was just past the mart and directed us upstream, on a track to a gate, and the green fields beyond.

The sign at MR 91/946252 was a well defined starting point for this stretch of the Pennine Way, and the path, as it roughly followed the Yorkshire bank of the Tees, needed no further directional instructions. As the river meandered the path tended to keep on a fairly steady north westerly course. Three river bridges were passed, Scoberry, Wynch and Holwick Head, and the path lay close to the river bank in these areas. After Holwick Head bridge the opposite bank was well-wooded and the roar of High Force Waterfall could be heard. Shortly after High Force a large quarry marred the opposite bank, and the path drifted away from the river after Skyer Beck, a tributary coming in from the south. Our path took us over a slight knoll with stunted trees and on to Cronkley Bridge.

The walk up the River Tees was the most idyllic of the entire Pennine Way. In places we could only see the river through dense foliage, the water shining silver as it made wide sweeps across the valley bottom. In other places high banks allowed us to look down on the river between the trunks of trees precariously growing out of the near vertical slopes. Brilliant sunshine gave the water a jewel-like sparkle, and birds and butterflies were everywhere. Across the river we could see the road that shared the valley, and a few cars and very occasional bus. The village of Newbiggin sheltered in the lee of the steep hills that rose to the north, and a small footbridge offered access to the village. In places, the rocky banks of the river, especially on the northern side, were composed of expanses of flat grey stone, with round potholes filled with water, rather like varying sizes of wash hand basins. It was easy to visualise trapped stones being whirled round and round, slowly enlarging these gigantic pock marks, as winter floods changed this tranquil water into a raging torrent.

After Scoberry Bridge the water channel seemed to narrow and the banks of grey limestone were more restrictive. The verges of the river were well covered with trees and the picturesque Wynch Bridge was delicately suspended over the placid water. As we moved to the centre of the span the bridge swayed to our every step, but stout steel supports and side rails gave absolute confidence. As the river flowed languidly many feet below, it was hard to realise that prior to the construction of the massive Cow Green reservoir upstream, the winter floods washed over the spot where we stood. In those days this river ran wild, filling the river bed and spreading wide on either side, but now, even in winter storms, the river is comparatively docile.

Above the bridge we reached Low Force, a more open landscape, with water cascading down a jumbled staircase of rock. The water glistened in the sun, a rusty, brownish tint told us of the presence of peat in the collecting area miles upstream, and we thought of our experiences crossing Teeshead on a previous walk. The weather and scenery were perfect, picnickers were gathering on the river banks, and cameras were clicking in all directions. We continued upstream.

The next bridge, Holwick Head, did not have the charm of Wynch Bridge. This was a plain girdered affair, with a mid-river support. The utilitarian aspect of the bridge was offset by the still water surrounding it, and the clear reflections. The clear blue skies, the reflected blue in the water and the grassy banks made it a very restful spot. In a further half mile we reached High Force. Before we reached it, passing through low trees and bushes, we could hear the crash of the water as it forced its way through the narrow gap and dropped about sixty feet into the water-worn pit below. This much photographed spot is always spectacular. The rugged promontory in the centre of the channel, and the backcloth of trees covering the banks beyond was beautiful, a truly calendar picture. We have never seen this fall when the river is in full spate but it must be a majestic sight when the water thunders down either side of the huge rocky central pillar, and possibly spills over the rock crest. We confess to being summertime walkers.

We climbed the high bank of the Tees gorge and the world changed. The far bank was still tree clad but beyond and above them was a cloud of dust. We could hear the clatter of quarrying machinery on the far bank, and we could see this horrible man-made scar. Our path, on the Yorkshire bank wound its way through juniper bushes and on to the next river bridge.

At Cronkley Bridge, with the quarry well behind us, we crossed to the opposite bank and headed on a Tees tributary, Harwood Beck, until we reached the next bridge, near New House Farm, and signs indicating the Pennine Way swinging almost due west. That was Saur Hill Bridge, and was the limit for this walk, so we turned and retraced our steps along the banks of the River Tees to Wynch Bridge, crossed the bridge and walked down the road to Newbiggin. Passing to the far end of the village we turned left up a minor, metalled road and, at the T junction headed to the right. This road, running southeast, high on the valley side, was followed down into Middleton, joining the B6277 to enter the village.

We debated at the Saur Hill Bridge. The alternatives were to strike out for the nearest point on the B6277 and follow the road back to Middleton, passing the High Force Hotel en route, possibly using river paths for some of the way, or to retrace our steps to Wynch Bridge. On such a pleasant summer's day the decision wasn't difficult. We have a marked aversion to main roads and traffic. This return walk was really a huge success: we followed the river bank, seeing things we had missed on the way up, and closing our eyes to the quarry across the river. There is so much beauty in this valley that no one could hope to see it all on one trip. We were almost sorry to reach Wynch Bridge. After the bridge we were forced to yield to a short stretch of road walking, but we knew that ahead was a long stretch of traffic-free road. We had decided, while walking, that we would not follow the main road directly to Middleton but would take the by-road.

The climb from the valley road up through Newbiggin was steep. At the T junction in the village there was a seat, with closely cropped grass around it, and a tethered pony acting as unpaid lawnmower. The climb became steeper as we progressed, and the rests became frequent, our legs were getting tired, but at each resting point the view improved. Resting at the top of our climb, and practically on the crest of the hill, we had a wonderful panoramic view of Teesdale. The road and the river in the foreground, were about 500 feet below us, against rocky scars beyond we could see Holwick. Almost due south was the trig point on Harter Fell, and the copse of hill-top trees at Kirk Carrion. This wonderful view alone was worth the seventeen miles that we had covered before we climbed into the car and headed back to our riverside haven.

WALK 23

SAUR HILL TO CAULDRON SNOUT

(A circular walk of ten miles)

We couldn't really expect glorious sunshine for every walk. We had been warned by seasoned walkers of the atrocious weather conditions that had prevailed when they had tackled the Pennine Way, and yet, in the main, we had successfully dodged the rain for most of our walks. But as we left our caravan site and drove up the B6277, past High Force, the grey sky seemed to get heavier and more depressing. When we reached Langdon Beck we turned sharply left and crossed Harwood Beck and headed for Cow Green reservoir. The car park (MR 91/815308) was empty and a cold breeze swept in from the huge expanse of water. We checked that our waterproofs were readily available and headed back, on foot, the way we had arrived.

The unfenced road, running almost due east, joined the minor road and we continued in the same direction until we reached Harwood Beck. We ignored the farm road leading to Widdybank Farm, but took a footpath that followed the general direction of the stream, Langdon Beck. In less than a mile we reached the track that links New House Farm and Wheysike and crosses the beck by Saur Hill Bridge. Signs on the bridge confirm that this is the Pennine Way. We turned west, heading back towards the Tees, on vague field paths in the direction of Widdybank Farm, with stiles and farm gates as our guide. Leaving the farm we dropped down to the river bank, with Cronkley Scar opposite, and passed through Holmwath pasture. Next came the Falcon Clints, a jumble of rocks and boulders before we passed on to Cauldron Snout.

The walk from Saur Hill Bridge, through grassy fields, to Widdybank was a pleasant stroll which was marred only by the dull, heavy skies and the rather cold north west breeze. As we neared the banks of the River Tees we knew, from our books, that we were in a botanist's paradise. Bird's eye primrose, blue gentian, yellow saxifrage, shrubby cinquefoil and the small Teesside violets can all be found in this area in season. If the sun had been shining and the breeze a gentle zephyr we would probably have lingered and found

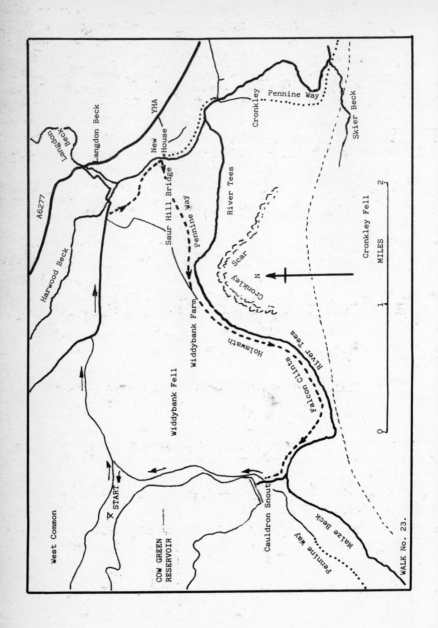

WALK No. 23.

West Common

COW GREEN RESERVOIR

START

Widdybank Fell

Cauldron Snout

Maize Beck

Pennine Way

Falcon Clints

Holmwath

River Tees

Widdybank Farm

Pennine Way

Scar

Cronkley

N

Cronkley Fell

MILES
0   1   2

Harwood Beck

A6277

Langdon Beck

Langdon Beck

YHA

New House

Saur Hill Bridge

Pennine Way

River Tees

Cronkley

Pennine Way

Skier Beck

a specimen or two, but threatening skies prompted us to keep moving.

We knew of the hazards of Falcon Clints from a previous walk in this area, when we met a very special walker. On that occasion we had strolled down from Cow Green to Cauldron Snout in bright sunshine and were sitting on rocks having our picnic. In the distance we saw a bearded figure with very short shorts and apparently very long legs. He was striding easily through the rocks, and it was obvious that he was a very experienced walker. We were pleased when, with the usual walker's friendliness, he stopped to chat. He casually mentioned that he was on a training walk—a mere thousand miles. We gasped in amazement and he then told us that his next walking project was round the coast of Britain—a massive seven thousand miles. His name was John Merrill, we already had a couple of his small walking books, and later we were to hear him speak of that gigantic walk. Of course, we also now have his book "Turn right at Land's End". Meeting and talking with this great walker probably created in us the urge to tackle bigger things.

On this walk, in miserable weather, we met no one. We scrambled through nature's dolerite rockery at Falcon Clints, balancing on some rocks, slipping in between others. It was the perfect recipe for sprained ankles and skinned shinbones. We could only admire the scenery across the river when we stopped to rest. When we were moving all our attention had to be directed at our feet. As the rocks thinned a little progress was easier and we could hear the tumbling waters of Cauldron Snout. We knew then that the hazardous part of the walk was almost ended. The rocky outcrops of Cronkley Scar changed to heather and bilberry bushes on the bank opposite, and Maize Beck joined the main river. Ahead the white, foaming water of Cauldron Snout crashed over the jagged rocky stairway, and the spray was caught in the breeze and blew in our direction.

We found a sheltered niche in the rocks, our feet were almost in the water, but the wind passed overhead and we were out of the spray, so we had our picnic. Slight breaks in the grey clouds came and went, and our hopes for a change in the weather faltered, but even in inclement weather there is still considerable beauty at Cauldron Snout.

We climbed up the slope from the waterfall to the man-made barrier which held back millions of gallons of water, and then on a good, metalled road back to our car at the completely deserted car park.

91

As we prepared to leave our sheltered spot amid the rocks we realised that all the moisture that was in the air was not spray. At last the Weather God had made a decision, it was raining. Out came the waterproof jackets and leggings and, like two deep-sea fishermen, we headed for the car park. Having finally broken, the weather knew no bounds. The strength of the wind increased to near gale force, the surface of the reservoir was a mass of white caps on miniature waves. The rain resembled knitting needles as it was driven forcibly into our faces, and the temperature dropped several degrees. This was Pennine weather. Our early morning thoughts of a walk on the banks of the reservoir, and up the valley to the Moor nature reserve were forgotten. It was a relief to reach the car and discard our waterproofs, and head for the warmth and comfort of our caravan, at Middleton-in-Teesdale.

Another ten miles had been added to our overall total. A sign on Saur Hill Bridge had stated how many miles of the Pennine Way had been completed, we wondered of how and by whom it had been measured. Our pedometer told us that we had walked about 300 miles, but we knew that only about half of that was on the Pennine way, but at least we were now past the halfway mark, and we were contented.

CAULDRON SNOUT TO HIGH CUP NICK

(A circular walk of fourteen miles)

Our previous walk had ended in heavy rain and we knew that this section of the Pennine Way could be boggy in places and included fording Maize Beck, so we decided to have a lazy day, seeing the local beauty spots, driving on deserted country roads or sitting in idyllic surroundings just listening to the multitude of country sounds. We hoped that the warm sun and the zephyr breeze would dry out the path and that the water level in the Maize Beck would fall to make our crossing easier. Most Pennine Way writers warned that the walk, with wild moorlands rising on either side could be the loneliest on the entire Way. We thought back to some of the stretches that we had covered between Edale and Hebden Bridge and wondered just what we were embarking upon.

Another fine day dawned and without hesitation we donned our walking gear. The nearest car park was the one previously used at Cow Green reservoir, we drove there, and parked in isolation.

We were forced to start along the same paths as we had finished our previous walk, heading south to the impressive damhead of the reservoir that was so completely out of keeping with the surrounding countryside. A bridge between the top of the falls and the concrete damhead is the start of this section of the Pennine Way and a lane, or cart track, led us to Birkdale Farm. We headed southwest from the farm, on a distinct path, and crossed a small stream, Grain Beck, in less than a quarter of a mile. Keeping on much the same bearing we climbed to the mine dumps at Moss Shop—shown on the map as Mine (dis)—and then followed a cairned route, which fluctuated to almost due west in places, to Maize Beck. We followed the north bank for a couple of hundred yards before we found a suitable crossing point and, using strategically placed stones managed to cross to the south bank. The path, with an occasional cairn was easy to follow right through to High Cup Nick.

We started out on this walk with some doubts and trepidation, but the glorious sunshine soon dispelled our fears. The reservoir looked peaceful and reflected the bright blue of the sky. Winchats

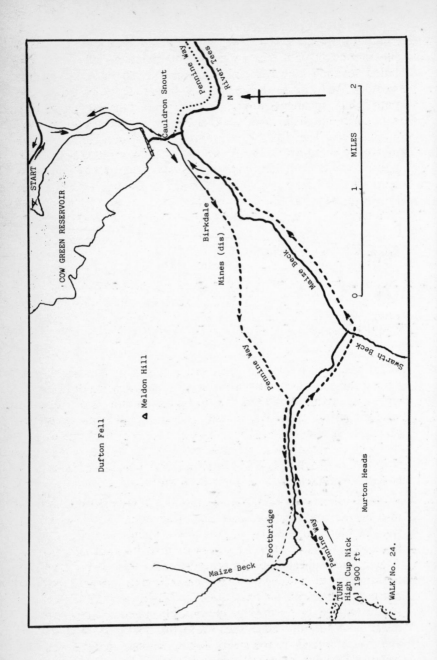

94

fluttered from bush to bush, and skylarks soared overhead, their rapid wingbeats pumping out a glorious melody. The horrible track of our previous, wet walk which led to the top of the falls, was now a pleasant sunlit path. The solid concrete damhead still jarred and failed to show any redeeming features, even in such glorious weather. We by-passed locked gates to head for Birkdale Farm. The path failed to match the awesome descriptions that we had read. It was a pleasant, distinct path, not the rough, boggy track that we had anticipated. The farm was certainly in a desolate area, we marvelled that anyone should live in such a remote spot, but the house looked occupied, and we presumed that the farmer must hold a key to unlock the Water Authority gate that straddles the only route between the farm and the car park. We wondered what would happen to unexpected car-borne visitors who had no key!

Having passed the farm, fording Grain Beck was easy. Large lumps of limestone provided adequate stepping stones and the other side was reached with dry feet. We climbed to the old mine dumps and saw the Moss Shop. We then changed our opinion of Birkdale Farm. That was a metropolis with first rate amenities compared with this lodging house for lead miners of years past. Conditions have certainly changed in the last 150 years.

We could see, Maize Beck meandering some 200 feet below. In a wide sweep it appeared to change direction and we were cutting off a huge corner as we followed a cairned path, dropping down to the riverbank. We explored the river in both directions and selected a spot for our crossing. We crossed, perilously balancing on water-polished, rocking stones. We were on the southern bank and we had two dry feet (between us) but the walking was easy and the surroundings idyllic, so we stopped and had a picnic on the water's edge, spreading our wet socks on the warm stones.

After a short walk on the southern bank the river swung sharply northwards, and lost itself in a small traversing valley, we left the river and headed almost southwest for a dip in the skyline that we knew was High Cup Nick. This was our most dramatic view to date. A giant mechanical digger appeared to have scooped out a steep but smooth-sided valley which stretched from its rocky inception at our feet to the fertile plains of the Eden Valley. A small, ribbon like stream twisted its way through the valley bottom and was lost in the distance. A few stunted bushes broke the symmetry of the valley and sheep grazed on the steep slopes. No cars could reach this beautiful lookout, it was well worth the walk.

This walk, truly, entailed returning by the same path as our outward journey, but the peaceful river bank tempted us and we followed the river bank much further than planned and joined the outward track at Birkdale Farm, and so back to the car park at Cow Green.

We reluctantly turned our backs on High Cup Nick and picked our way over pleasant grassy slopes to the banks of Maize Beck. We had walked from Cow Green to within sight of our turning point without seeing another living soul. The writers were right about the loneliness and the isolation, but the seclusion seemed to add to the natural beauty of the area. On reaching the river we chose to leave the official footpath where possibly other walkers would rob us of our seclusion, and we followed the bubbling, tumbling river. In places it spread out and shallowly passed round scores of scattered rocks, in other places it narrowed, and in one place it tumbled over a miniature waterfall. According to the map the official footpath ended at the county boundary, but we stuck to the bank of the river, sometimes on dry ground, and sometimes on boggy stretches, until we could see Birkdale Farm ahead. Then we headed back for the footpath and walked on to Cow Green and compared the solid concrete structure with the natural beauty of High Cup Nick. The afternoon sunshine lit up the path, bees buzzed, butterflies fluttered and birds sang. It was a different world to the finish of our previous walk.

And so back to camp, a meal and a quick pack up. Then over the beautiful B6276 to Brough, to join the A66 to Appleby where we found a pleasant little campsite at the village of Colby.

WALK 25
HIGH CUP NICK TO DUFTON
(An out and home walk of eleven miles)

The campsite at Colby had taken a lot of finding, it was tucked away on a very minor road, and has since been listed as a Camping and Caravanning Club Hideaway site. We could, of course, have stayed at one of the other listed sites in the Appleby–Dufton area, but we prefer the small, isolated sites, and this site was exactly that; we were the only people in residence. To reach the site we entered Appleby on the B6542 and found our way on to the B6260, and then took the Colby Moor road for about a mile. As the sun was setting we strolled down to the river bridge and into the village, and looked up at the hills that would be our walking area for our next two jaunts.

In the morning we made a quick trip round Appleby, just enough to allow us to do a little shopping and have a passing glimpse of the castle. Someday we must go back and look at this pleasant market town properly. Leaving the town we passed under the busy A66 and headed for Dufton which was the starting point of the walk. Knowing that this was only a ten or eleven mile walk we had time to look at this open-plan village. Parking was easy, wide grassy verges, a beautiful village green and a scarcity of traffic on this country road was a motorist's dream. The red sandstone cottages intrigued us, it was such a contrast to the dull grey, slatey dolomite rock of these northern Pennines. Quiet cottages, with dates in the seventeen hundreds, surrounded the green where young walkers from the nearby Youth Hostel were planning their walk.

We left the car at the east end of the village (MR 91/688252) and followed the road back to Town Head and a footpath sign on the left. A rough, stoney track led up the hillside, the climb becoming steeper as we progressed. After about two miles the lane ended and a footpath, cairned in places, continued to climb along the slopes of the steep sided valley, and finally to a craggy escarpment at the head of High Cup.

It was pleasant but warm work climbing up the steep lane from Dufton. Away to our left we could see the peculiar conical hills of Dufton Pike, Knock Pike and Brownber Hill, but the view ahead and to our right was impressive. The little stream, High Cup Gill,

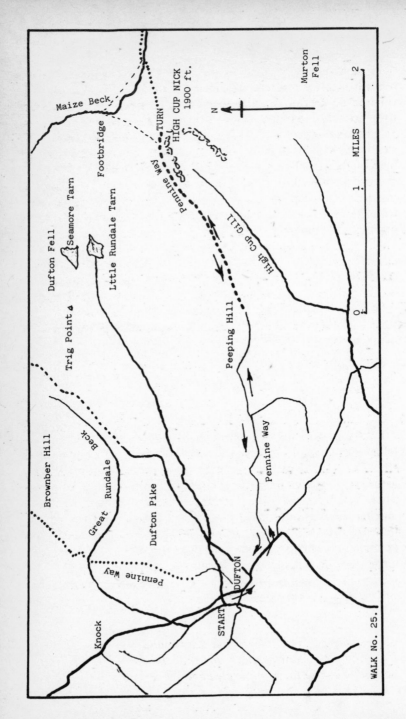

Maize Beck

Footbridge

Dufton Fell

Seamore Tarn

Little Rundale Tarn

Trig Point ▲

Brownber Hill

Great Rundale Beck

Dufton Pike

Knock

Pennine Way

DUFTON

START

TURN

Pennine Way

HIGH CUP NICK 1900 ft.

High Cup Gill

Peeping Hill

Pennine Way

Murton Fell

N

MILES
0   1   2

WALK No. 25.

98

wound its way along the valley bottom, sheep grazed precariously on the steep slopes and the way ahead we could see the rocky crags of High Cup Nick, the extremity of the previous walk. A farmhouse near the end of the lane provided refreshments, and we sat at a small table overlooking this wonderful panorama, and drank that irreplaceable cup of tea.

As we climbed the final stages of the path we watched a shepherd, with his dogs, collecting sheep from what appeared to be inaccessible small patches of pasture amid rugged crags. Not a sheep was missed as the two dogs, working without any apparent instructions, swept along the valley sides, and drove the sheep towards the tractor-mounted shepherd. Man and beast, nature and machine, all combined to give effortless efficiency.

The day was still young and we had time to scramble over the crags. Some of the vertical, column-like rocks stood almost 100 feet high and we searched for the ideal gap, which we presumed to be the Nick, to get an impressive photograph of this beautiful valley. The small white rivulet took our eyes through to the lush Eden Valley and from there to the hazy mountain range of Lakeland including Skiddaw and Coniston Old Man.

Our maps offered us no alternative route between Dufton and High Cup Nick so our return journey was an exact reversal of our outward trip, and without deviations, or a stop for a cup of tea, we returned to the village of Dufton.

Heading down the valley was even more dramatic. The ground fell away so rapidly, the sweep of the valley seemed so precise, the stream twisted and gleamed in the sun, and with the sheep all safely gathered, not a living thing moved in this wide expanse. Clumps of trees dotted the lush valley, and the heat haze clothed the far hills making them appear more distant and ethereal. Closer at hand there were further conical pikes, and the steep western slopes of the Pennine range. This was one of our shorter walks, with no difficult terrain, but it certainly was one of the most scenic.

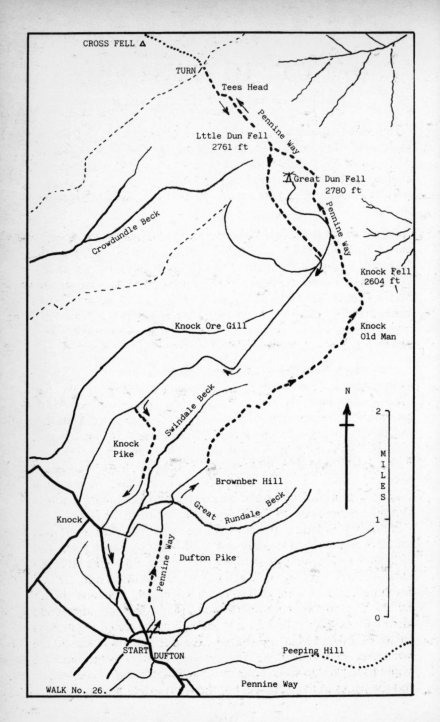

CROSS FELL △

TURN

Tees Head

Lttle Dun Fell
2761 ft

Pennine Way

△ Great Dun Fell
2780 ft

Pennine Way

Crowdundle Beck

Knock Fell
2604 ft

Knock Ore Gill

Knock
Old Man

Swindale Beck

N

Knock
Pike

2

M
I
L
E
S

Brownber Hill

Great Rundale Beck

1

Knock

Pennine Way

Dufton Pike

0

START DUFTON

Peeping Hill

WALK No. 26.

Pennine Way

100

DUFTON TO TEES HEAD

(A partly circular walk of sixteen miles)

This was the second walk to start at Dufton, with our caravan based at Colby, and we chose the same parking spot as before, (MR 91/688252). As we looked towards the mountains that rose so steeply, we thanked our lucky stars that we had another fine, sunny day, although there was a fairly strong breeze from the northeast.

We picked up the footpath near the pub and headed for the farm road to Coatsike. Field paths led almost due north to Great Rundale Beck and a further track, heading northeast, took us to Swindale Beck. A steep climb gradually levelled off and ahead we could see Knock Old Man, near to the summit of Green Fell. At the summit our path swung to the left on a bearing of about 330 degrees, but a compass was not necessary as we aimed directly for the radio mast on Great Dunn Fell.

The stretch from Dufton to Great Rundale Beck was a gentle stroll, and the old clapper bridge gave us a safe passage over the small stream, but as we climbed beyond there the terrain seemed to deteriorate. On the rising ground we scrambled over loose stones, and, as we crossed over tributaries of Rundale and Swindale becks, patches of sphagnum moss warned us of water underfoot. Looking back, Knock Pike looked like a small extinct volcano, with its sharp peak and even conical formation. It was in this area we passed a notice telling us the things that we must not do, but failing to tell us to climb up these beautiful hills and enjoy nature in the raw.

Following Swindale Beck we picked our way through small boulders and climbed steadily into a fairly strong northeaster, and the higher we got the stronger the wind became. Emerging on to the comparatively level top of Green Fell it seemed that a full gale had developed, and we were glad to reach Knock Old Man and shelter behind this solidly built cairn that dominated the immediate surroundings. This called for a break and we snuggled together in the lee of the Old Man and shared a flask of tea, and observed the wonderful view. The Lake District was clearly visible, and we would have liked to spread our map and identify the villages below and the peaks in the distance, but the wind would have none of it.

Knock Old Man—my old gal.

We had climbed about 2000 feet in the four or five miles from Dufton, and we had about the same distance to go to our turning point.

Our course lay directly towards the radio mast. This multi-girdered construction scarred the skyline but made navigation easy as we crossed the comparatively level limestone plateau. The jumbled rocks and narrow crevices made walking difficult, especially with the boisterous crosswind that now whistled in from Teesdale.

Heading directly towards the mast the ground lost a little height and then struck the tarmac service road to the radio station, but we used this road for only a very short distance before a finger post sent us up a rough path through coarse tussocky grass and peat, still heading directly towards the mast. We skirted the northeast side of the radio station on Great Dunn Fell, at a height of 2780 feet, and then on to Little Dun Fell which is only slightly lower. Across the dip ahead was Cross Fell, but our planned turning point was Tees Head, the watershed between the Tees to the east and Crowdundle Beck to the west. We walked northwest to our turning point.

Before we reached the service road to the radio station we had started to look for a suitable picnic spot. Somewhere out of the wind, where we could sit in comfort, preferably with a pleasant outlook. Sheltered spots were certainly hard to find on the windswept plateau and we had crossed the road before we found a grassy depression formed by a man-made trench running across the fall of the land. It didn't provide a very good viewpoint but it was sheltered and sunny, and we were hungry. We speculated on the original purpose of the wide ditch and have since found that it is called Dun Fell Hush, and was an artificial water course made by the lead miners to expose the mineral veins.

Having eaten and rested we again exposed ourselves to the gale force wind. It seemed to increase in ferocity as we crossed the flat top of Little Dun Fell and we found it better to link together to increase our stability as the wind was practically sweeping us off our feet. Our slow progress, which wasn't unusual, allowed two other walkers to catch up with us as we scrambled between tussocks of grass and heather down the peaty slopes to Tees Head.

They were an interesting couple. One was provisionally surveying a possible course for a mountain race, and the other, an Australian, was relishing the wildness of the Pennines. As we were planning a visit to Australia, my wife, Nancy, seized the opportunity to ask questions. They were following, deeply engrossed in their conversation, when our Australian friend stepped on to an expanse of black earth. We turned, hearing his shout, to find that he had sunk thigh deep into what looked like a patch of hard peat. We ran back and, between the two of us, pulled him out of the peat bog like a cork from a bottle. There was a look of amazement, almost fear, on his face which was greeted by the casual comment of my companion "Just shake yourself, it'll all drop off." The experience made us all much more careful and observant. Shortly after that we said goodbye to our erstwhile companions and headed back for the summit of Little Dun Fell.

The return to the crest of the hills was on much the same path as the descent, but reaching the top we tried to lose a little height on the leeside of the mountain to avoid the high winds. We skirted the radio station and picked up the service road, and followed the tarmac for easy walking. The original plan was to leave this road and follow Sink Beck round Knock Pike, but we changed our plan and followed the road turning sharp left on a track as we approached Knock Pike. Skirting round the Pike we joined Swindale Beck and then a country lane that took us to Knock. A quiet unclassified road took us back to Dufton.

Our legs began to ache as we climbed away from Teeshead. We were thankful that at the top of Great Dun Fell we would have downhill all the way to Dufton. Joining the service road we soon lost height and being in the lee of the mountain the force of the wind abated. Walking was easy. We looked at the vague footpath that ran close to Sink Beck and visualised stretches of water-sodden moss. Our tired legs prompted us to keep to the road for another mile, and we found an easy, grassy footpath through the col at Knock Pike. From there it was comfortable walking to the hamlet of Knock and then to the car at Dufton.

We had walked sixteen miles and reached our highest point so far. The map said 2780 feet but we estimated that the ups and downs on the way had taken us well over 3000 feet. Our legs confirmed this, they were tired, but our spirits were high, we had completed another section of the Pennine Way. On the following day we hitched our caravan and headed for home.

We knew that it was going to be several months before we would make a further assault on the Pennine Way. During the year we had had three sessions of about ten to twelve days when we had been in the vicinity of the Way, and we had walked on twenty six days and covered about 330 miles. We planned to resume our journeying in the Spring.

The winter months were passed talking about the past and the future and, as with most walkers, looking at the slides. We planned for the next year when we would start by climbing to the top of Cross Fell and resume our journey, cross the border and the Cheviots and reach Kirk Yetholm to finish the Pennine Way. Easter couldn't come quickly enough.

TEES HEAD TO GARRIGILL

(An out and home walk of sixteen miles)

As Spring approached we prayed for a fine Easter, we still had about one third of the Pennine Way to walk, and to add to our forebodings it was the northern part where the weather could be more unpredictable. We were working to a deadline as we had already purchased our tickets for a flight to Australia at the end of June, and we would therefore miss all the summer weather in the U.K. Our minds were a jumble of planned walks between Tees Head and Kirk Yetholm and drives between Melbourne and Cairns. As Easter arrived we prepared the caravan and headed for Alston. Throughout our walks we never booked ahead for a camp site, preferring to see the spot before committing ourselves. We followed the same practice and drove into Alston and found a spot near the town centre, on a narrow neck of land by the river. The facilities were not oustanding but were adequate, and the location was ideal.

On the Thursday prior to Easter we drove to Garrigill in Spring sunshine and parked the car in this quiet village. The countryside looked so clean and fresh, buds were bursting and the birds were singing and our spirits were high.

We picked up the Pennine Way sign at the far end of the village (MR 86/743413) and followed the path in a generally southerly direction climbing up a walled track. The official path was well signed in this area but we noted that practically all signs were erected for the benefit of south to north walking. After a mile or so the track veered to our right but our path went straight ahead, climbing steeply over open country. We struck the same walled track about a mile further on. The path went over the summit of Pikeman Hill and along the upper, western slopes of Long Man Hill to the start of the old mine workings. These mine workings became more obvious as the track veered to the west and eventually passed by sparsely furnished Greg's Hut. This is a bothy type shelter where walkers can find refuge and overnight cover in inclement weather. Half a mile or so past the hut, ignoring the well defined path straight ahead, our Pennine Way path headed off to our left directly to the summit of Cross Fell.

The climb was enjoyable, the air was fresh, the temperature was

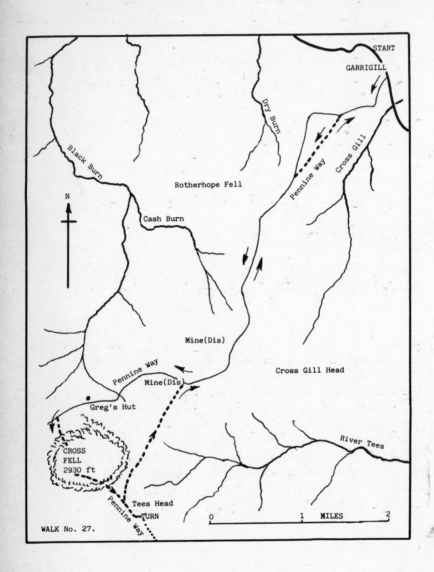

START
GARRIGILL

Dry Burn

Pennine Way

Cross Gill

Black Burn

Rotherhope Fell

N

Cash Burn

Mine(Dis)

Cross Gill Head

Pennine Way

Mine(Dis)

Greg's Hut

River Tees

CROSS
FELL
2930 ft

Pennine Way

Tees Head
TURN

WALK No. 27.

0   1   MILES   2

not too high and the sun was shining brightly. Passing through the mine workings we wandered from the track, and pictured the activity of this area some 150 years ago, when the mines were in full production, and the place would be thronged with men and horses. The rough tracks were coated with stone chippings, many of which could be polished to reveal attractive colourings. We collected a couple of stones as mementoes of our visit. As we made our final assault on Cross Fell we picked our way through loose scree and rocky outcrops, and the cooler breeze reminded us that we were almost 3000 feet above sea level. This was the highest point of the Pennine Way.

Looking to the southeast the radio mast on Dunn Fell made an unattractive scar on the skyline. In the depression between was the deceptively boggy ground that had trapped our Australian friend some six months ago. As usual, on high points, we sat and looked around. Cow Green reservoir sparkled in the sun, it looked quite attractive from there. It looked so close and yet we had walked a considerable distance since we parked the car on its banks and walked by Cauldron Snout at the end of last summer. In the midst of the huge, seemingly desolate landscape was Moor House nature reserve, and away in the distance the road and river winding their way to Middleton-in-Teesdale.

The summit of Cross Fell was not our ultimate target for this walk, so we headed southeast directly for Little Dunn Fell to the lowest point in the depression, where we had turned on our previous walk. Retracing our steps towards the summit our map indicated a crossing path which, by taking this to our right, we would miss the scree slopes of the fell and rejoin the Pennine Way at the mine workings. We searched for this and scrambled along the slopes but the boggy ground below forced us up into the scree and skirting along the edge of this we eventually found our way back to the mine workings. From there the navigation was simple, covering exactly the same ground as the outward trip, and losing height all the way.

For anyone following in our footsteps for this section my one word of advice is—don't. The effort of scrambling round the slopes of Cross Fell searching for that elusive path, and dodging extensive boggy patches, was far greater than climbing back to the cairn. Apart from that, the return trip was perfect. Going we had had the mountain mass ahead of us, and the watershed and the depression at Tees Head was a lifeless, desolate vista. Returning we could see the valley, with Garrigill in the deep recess, and green fields and traces of civilisation. But our real pleasure came from knowing that we had resumed where we had left off and that another dozen pleasant walks were ahead of us.

We could hardly believe our pedometer which told us we had wandered sixteen miles. We were thankful that we had kept active through the winter months with regular weekend walks.

WALK 28

ALSTON TO LAMBLEY CHAPEL

(A one-way walk of twelve miles)

The camp site did little to encourage us to lounge about, and, despite the heavy cloud, damp atmosphere and unsatisfactory weather forecasts we decided that we must press on. It was surprising how the weather had changed overnight, but this was a Saturday on a Bank Holiday weekend and we had grown to expect adverse weather on such days. The short walk, from Garrigill to Alston was being deferred to a later date when we would use part of the day to move to our next camping area. We had checked the bus timetables and had found that there was a suitable bus to carry us back to the camp site, so, in this instance, we could embark on a one-way walk. We had to reach the bus stop at Lambley Chapel by five thirty to return to camp.

We left the car parked on the caravan site (MR 86/715468), packed our rucksacks, with the waterproofs readily available, and crossed the river to the old railway station. Our footpath ran alongside the lines.

Following the railway line, in a northerly direction, we recrossed the river after about three quarters of a mile, and picked up a footpath across a field to the buildings at Harbut Lodge. From there a definite track led to the main road (A689). Turning north and then west we crossed the road following the Pennine Way sign. We climbed slightly and then dropped into the valley of Gilderdale Burn and followed down stream for a few hundred yards. A well defined path led us round the old Roman Fort of Whitley Castle, and then re-crossed the tarmac road. Our path then ran between the river and the road for almost two miles, actually joining the road to enter Slaggyford.

We had barely started our walk from the old railway station when the forecasters' threats became reality, and the rain started. We could still see the caravan, dry and secure, behind us, but we were determined to complete this section which, on the map, did not look very exciting. We sheltered in a hut and struggled into our waterproofs and, undaunted, headed northwards. There was no doubt that the weather dampened our appreciation of the old Roman fort. Normally we would have stopped and talked, and

109

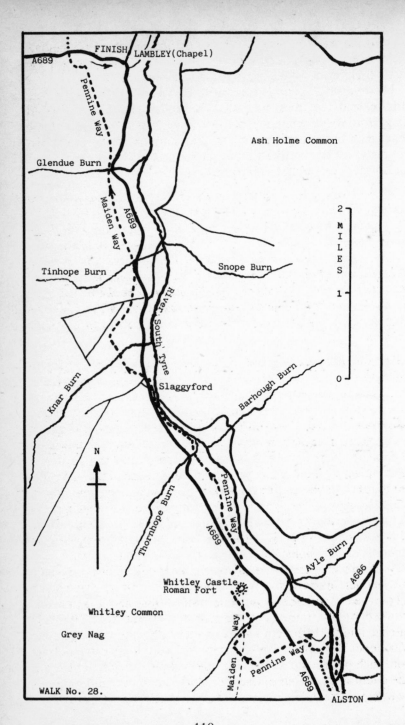

FINISH LAMBLEY(Chapel)

A689

Pennine Way

Ash Holme Common

Glendue Burn

Maiden Way

A689

Tinhope Burn

Snope Burn

River South Tyne

Knar Burn

Slaggyford

Barhough Burn

N

Thornhope Burn

Pennine Way

A689

Ayle Burn

Whitley Castle
Roman Fort

A686

Whitley Common

Grey Nag

Maiden Way

Pennine Way

A689

WALK No. 28.

ALSTON

2
M
I
L
E
S
1

0

110

created mental pictures of ancient warriors in togas and sandals dashing along the Maiden Way in chariots. We just tried to stop the water trickling down the necks of our waterproofs.

The riverside walk was less trying. The rain had eased to a fine drizzle, and the trees concealed the dull skies. As we entered Slaggyford we were tempted to enter a cosy hostelry and refresh the inner man but struggling out, and then into, our waterproofs discouraged us. We had flasks and sandwiches in our packs and we had always been addicted to picnicking.

A small road on our left took us out of Slaggyford, and we crossed open fields with dry stone walls, following close to the old railway line, and touching the main road again at the bridge over Thinhope Burn. Once across the burn we left the road on a marked path climbing the bank to our left, but never losing sight of the road on our right. We approached the road again to cross Glendue Burn and then, over heather clad slopes, northward to strike the road once more after it had swung westwards at Lambley Chapel. The Pennine Way went straight across, but we turned right and headed for the small bus shelter at Lambley Chapel.

The weather had worsened as we left Slaggyford, as if trying to force us to cancel our picnic. Wet walks have little to redeem them, and this was following the usual pattern, but the clock told us it was time to stop and eat. We found a reasonably high stone wall and crouched down on the sheltered side. With a red umbrella raised overhead to offer additional protection we ate soggy sandwiches and washed them down with hot tea. We appreciated that hardened Pennine Way walkers would despise us for the use of the umbrella, but a little episode at Hebden Bridge (see walk eight) on another Bank Holiday weekend, had prompted my wife to vow that in really wet weather she would walk with an umbrella. She justified this with a statement by the well-known A. W. that he carried an umbrella on occasions. We felt that we were in good company.

As usually happens, within twenty minutes of finishing our picnic the weather improved; a fresh breeze and a rather watery sun encouraged us to remove our waterproofs. If we had had previous knowledge of our route we would probably have delayed our picnic and had it in the complete shelter of a tunnel that took the Pennine Way under the old railway line, but various odours often detract from such places and at least we had had pure unadulterated air. The damp spots on our clothes soon dried, and our spirits rose as we tramped over Glendue Fell and on to Hartleyburn Common.

"Aren't humans funny?"

In the comparative warmth and comfort of a small bus shelter we ate the last of our food, drank the rest of our tea, and waited. Buses are infrequent on that route, but we were cheered by the knowledge that we had completed another stage of our walk. The ride back was dry and comfortable and the morrow was another day.

LAMBLEY TO GREAT CHESTERS

(A one way walk of fifteen miles)

The fickleness of the English Spring weather was in evidence as we woke on the morrow of our wet walk to Lambley. The sun was shining, a fresh breeze was blowing which moved the branches and a blackbird was singing a finale to the dawn chorus. We breakfasted quickly and packed our bags. This walk was to start at Lambley, and we used the car to get there, but a service bus would bring us back from Haltwhistle to Lambley. It was Sunday and we were planning to catch the last bus sometime before six o'clock.

Slaggyford which had looked depressing in the rain now appeared to be an attractive village, and we noticed caravans amid the trees, and children noisily splashing in the river. We passed the road junction at Lambley Chapel, the roads were almost devoid of traffic, and a wide verge against a red brick wall provided an ideal parking place for a day long stay. We knew that ahead of us was another lowland walk and deep down we were both yearning for open moorlands and soggy peat.

Our walk started at the crossing of the A689 by the Pennine Way (MR 86/663586) about half a mile west of Lambley Chapel road junction and our footpath headed slightly west of north. The distinct path with frequent signs was easy to follow as it twisted its way across Hartley Burn, heading for Batey Shield. A minor road was crossed in a dip at Kellah Burn and continuing northwest we crossed Wain Rigg and passed close to the trig point on Blenkinsopp Common. After crossing under the power lines a sharp right turn took us back under the same lines on a small walled track leading to Todholes. After another 500 yards our path swung northwards to pass under the power lines again and then on to the A69 trunk road.

In retrospect we found this part of the walk uninspiring. The weather was kind, the terrain was gentle and the route was easily followed and we felt that we had really left the Pennines behind. Our walking boots and packs appeared almost out of place in such sedate and civilised surroundings. We had spotted the almost continuous stream of cars, with very occasional heavy lorry, snaking

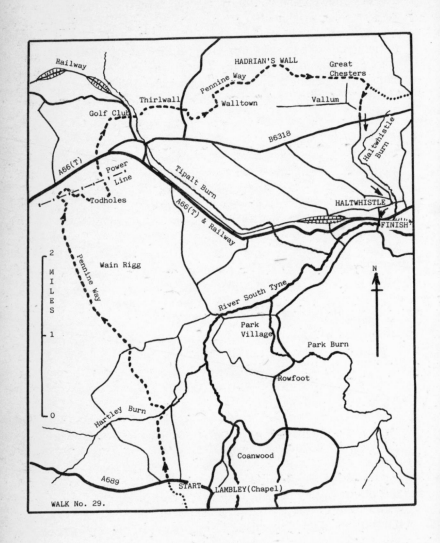

Railway

HADRIAN'S WALL

Great Chesters

Thirlwall

Pennine Way

Golf Club

Walltown

Vallum

B6318

A66(T)

Power Line

Tipalt Burn

Haltwhistle Burn

Todholes

A66(T) & Railway

HALTWHISTLE

FINISH

2 MILES 1 0

Pennine Way

Wain Rigg

River South Tyne

N

Park Village

Park Burn

Rowfoot

Hartley Burn

Coanwood

A689

START

LAMBLEY(Chapel)

WALK No. 29.

114

along the A69 half an hour before we reached the road, and we were not surprised to find road works and traffic control adding to the congestion. Non-walking, inconsiderate road makers had removed the Pennine Way signs, and obliterated any footpaths, and we scrambled up a muddy embankment and searched around for our path. Eventually we found a track and wended our way over a golf course and past the club house, wondering if we were trespassing. We retraced our steps for a short way and found the official path running alongside some ancient earthworks to lead us to the crossing of the B6318 and the main railway line.

After crossing the A69 and the roadworks the official path was slightly east of north and struck the Vallum (earthwork) after about half a mile. The long distance footpath turned right there, but there is a public right of way to the club house lane. We crossed the road and the railway line to Thirlwall Castle. From there the path was distinct, following the wall in an easterly direction, with frequent descents and climbs. After about two and a half miles Great Chesters was reached and we picked up a right of way that joined a track leading to the B6318. We crossed this road and in a little over a mile entered Haltwhistle and found the bus station.

On reaching Hadrian's Wall we found that we were joining vast numbers of people out for a Sunday stroll. They wore casual clothing and sandals, cameras were clicking, and pretty girls posed against solid Roman stonework. Binoculars were trained over the valley to the north to Thirlwall Common and beyond. We saw no other Pennine Way walkers, we, in muddy boots and walking breeches were the oddities, and the casual lightly clad folk were the norm.

We had thought that the walk along the wall would be easy, but we found that we were constantly climbing short, steep mounds, then dropping equally sharply down the other side. Our legs were telling us that we had done enough as we neared Great Chesters, and to further dampen our spirits, clouds had covered the blue sky and a fine drizzle forced us to don our waterproofs.

Our watches told us that we must not dawdle if we were to catch the last bus from Haltwhistle to Lambley Chapel. Our body heat rose as, still in waterproofs, we strode out for the small town. Reaching the built-up area we were told that the bus station was just round the corner, and then again just round the corner, and so on. It was with a sigh of relief that we finally found it beyond the railway line, and we had five minutes to spare.

On the ride home we decided that if public transport was to be used it was preferable to use it on the outward journey rather than have a deadline at the end of a long walk. The effortless bus ride and the car drive back to Alston was a welcome relief for tired legs.

GARRIGILL TO HARBUTT LODGE

(A one way walk of six miles)

Easter weekend was rapidly passing, it was Monday, a Bank Holiday, but the shops in Alston were ready to accept business from the passing tourist or the resident clientele. We didn't know which category we were in but we took advantage of a "short walk" day to replenish our larder. The steep, cobbled streets were still fairly quiet. A few locals were afoot and, unlike their town cousins, they were ready to acknowledge and speak to all who passed by.

A relative, who lived in Nenthead, had expressed a desire to help with transport. She had already supplied us with the public transport information, but also offered to ferry us to Garrigill to the start of the short walk from there to Harbutt Lodge. In bright sunshine we were deposited next to the Pennine Way notice board and with a lighter pack than usual we headed for the bridge over the South Tyne River (MR 86/743413).

The route was unmistakable. It followed close to the river heading downstream, on the left bank for a little over a mile, and then crossed the river near Sillyhall and climbed the bank to Bleagate, cutting off a sweep in the watercourse. We then dropped back to the river bank, and did not wander far from it, until we reached the main road on the southern outskirts of Alston. The main road bridge took us, once more, to the left bank, and a sign guided us across fields to Harbutt Lodge. The Pennine Way swung to the left at the Lodge, but we picked up a footpath of a previous walk, bearing right to re-cross the river and join the old railway back to Alston.

The peaceful tranquillity of this walk was unsurpassed. The sleepy little village of Garrigill sets the style. The country pub, the little shop, the leisurely pace of life gives absolute serenity. The river bubbles gently over a stony bed, and a vast range of plants grow at the water's edge. A dipper bobs from stone to stone, his white breastplate gleaming in the sunshine, and in a still by-water a moorhen busily forages for nesting material among the overhanging vegetation. The native birds had started their mating calls and for four miles or more we were never without the melodious song

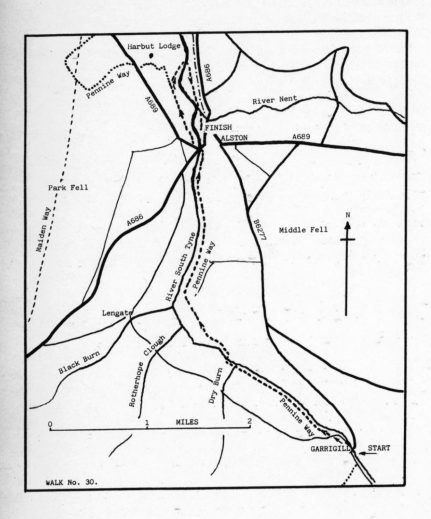

WALK No. 30.

118

of the blackbird, the song thrush, the robin, or the strident notes of the little wren.

Later in the year the valley abounds with flowers, we were able to find patches of delicate, miniature wild pansies and violets—both purple and white. Primroses and celandines dotted the banks, and the leaves of the bluebells were making a solid ground cover, ready for a carpet of blue.

But all good things come to an end, we couldn't avoid the traffic on the main road bridge over the river, and the escape across the fields to Harbutt Lodge was mundane after the beauties of the river valley. We were back at the camp in time for a picnic lunch outside our caravan, and then we prepared to move. This short walk could be practically doubled in length by using a little used minor road through Leadgate to Garrigill to make a circular walk.

The car and caravan journey to Haltwhistle was only short but after Lambley became somewhat devious as we tried to avoid the narrow lanes. Passing through Coanwood, Rowfoot and Park Village we entered Haltwhistle from the west on the A69. Dodging under the railway we turned left on a small lane to find a first class caravan site called Seldom Seen. Widely placed pitches, well-mown grass, a few trees and friendly neighbours—we were content for the rest of the day.

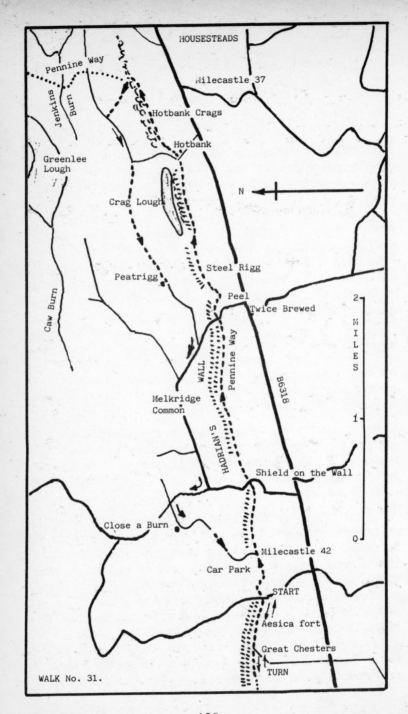

HOUSESTEADS

Milecastle 37

Pennine Way

Jenkins Burn

Hotbank Crags

Hotbank

Greenlee Lough

Crag Lough

N

Caw Burn

Steel Rigg

Peatrigg

Peel

Twice Brewed

2

M
I
L
E
S

WALL

Pennine Way

B6318

Melkridge Common

HADRIAN'S

1

Shield on the Wall

Close a Burn

Milecastle 42

0

Car Park

START

Aesica fort

Great Chesters

TURN

WALK No. 31.

120

WALK 31

GREAT CHESTERS TO HOTBANK CRAGS

(A circular walk of fourteen miles)

The holiday weekend was over and to prove it the weather had settled into pleasant sunshine, with only a slight breeze ruffling the leaves and cooling the brow. A few powder puff clouds moved slowly across the celestial dome and the verdict was a perfect day for a walk. A ten minute drive from the site at Haltwhistle and we were picking a parking spot in the almost unoccupied area near Hadrian's Wall at MR 86/712666, near to Great Chesters.

We had left the Wall two days previously in depressing drizzle, and dashed, almost despondently, for a bus to Haltwhistle. Now the bright morning sunshine, fresh, untired legs and a leisurely approach made the Wall an attractive and interesting object. We wandered around the remains of the once major fort of Aesica, near to Great Chesters Farm, and tried to imagine the scene with up to one thousand soldiers being stationed there in Roman Days. We knew that the wall, now a few feet high, and in places non-existent, was then up to twenty feet high, and stretched from coast to coast, much further than the eye could see.

The car park was a few hundred yards east of our previous turning point, so we followed the Pennine Way westwards, close to the Wall to the old fort (Aesica) and then retraced our steps and continued past Milecastle 42 and over Winshields. We passed Peel and Milecastle 39 and along the line of the Wall to Hotbank Crags.

Navigation was certainly the least of our problems on this part of the walk. The broad wall with a well-worn path close to it could not be missed, but the walk was far from level, steep descents and climbs were frequent. After a couple of miles we reached Winshields, the highest point of the Wall at 1230 feet. The clear weather and good visibility allowed us to look south to Cross Fell, and the end of the Pennines, and away to the west we could see the blue of the Irish Sea as it stretched into the Solway Firth.

At the road crossing, near Peel, a few more day trippers joined the path, but many only walked up to Milecastle 39 and then retreated. In places ladder stiles had been erected and paths had been well gravelled, but some slopes were very steep. And as we passed along Highshields we could look down on Crag Lough, the still waters reflecting the blue of the sky. There was little to see at Milecastle 38 but we had felt the ghostly presence of those Roman soldiers in the turrets and castles along the wall. There was a temptation to move on to Housesteads, but we stopped at a deep cutting through the crags, the ordnance survey map does not name it but we knew that it was Rapishaw Gap, the point where the Pennine Way left the Wall. We found a good comfortable viewpoint on Hotbank Crags and had our picnic.

The Pennine Way turns almost due north at Rapishaw Gap but we were leaving the Pennine Way, so we picked up a footpath running slightly west of north. This passed over flat land to strike a farm track leading to Hotbank Farm, we followed this westwards, leaving the track when it swung to the south. Keeping well to the north of the lough we aimed for a building about six hundred yards away and then kept straight on to pick up another farm track at Peat-Rigg. This soon brought us out on to a minor road and we turned away from the crags and the Wall. Our route continued on the road to a T junction, ignoring one or two lanes on our right, and there we turned right to Close-a-Burns. Shortly after crossing a stream and passing a chapel, we followed a track to our left which took us back to the car park.

It was a relief to get on to flat land after the sharp undulations of the path by the Wall. As we looked back at the line of crags, in places we could see the Wall, and it was obvious what a good defensive line it was that the Romans had established 2000 years ago. At its peak it was estimated that twenty thousand troops were stationed along the wall, and seventeen major forts were manned along the seventy three miles fortification, from Wallsend to Bowness, and every natural defence feature had been used to its full advantage.

The quiet paths and narrow roads that we followed from Hotbank Crags back to the car park gave us plenty of time for contemplation, and the opportunity to stand back and look at the Wall. On the two miles or so that we spent on a narrow tarmac road we didn't see a single car, and in the hedgerows and fields we didn't see a single marauding Scot to challenge the impregnability of the Wall.

We returned to Seldom Seen to dream of Roman Legions.

WALK 32

HOTBANK CRAGS TO
WARKS BURN

(An out and home walk of eighteen miles)

We chose the "B" road route to start our day's outing, picking up the B6318, whose straightness makes it look so uninteresting on the map. It gave us a fast run to the car park at Housesteads, where our walk was scheduled to begin. This was one of the places on the Wall that we had previously visited. The walk ahead of us was estimated at 16 miles and we did not feel that we had time to linger and see the Roman remains.

Housesteads, the Roman fort of Vercovicium, along with many other places along the Wall, justifies a special visit when one has time to browse over the relics, ponder the mysteries, and draw mental pictures of those far off days. There is a wonderful museum with plans, maps and models which help to put flesh on the bones of history. Signs and notice boards indicate the various points of interest, and the official HMSO guide is a wealth of information. I had always imagined swarthy Italians manning these forts, and longing for the sunshine of Rome. I was surprised to find that this fort was probably manned by one thousand Tungrians who came from Belgium.

There are four massive gateways to the fort in which one can still find the Commandant's House, the barracks and the granary. Outside the walls were the civilian settlements with all the amenities of a small town, shops, taverns and houses. One of the houses is called Murder House; the remains of a man found buried under the floor had part of a knife blade still in his ribs.

But all that was in the past, on this visit we passed through the fort, glancing casually at the wheel ruts left by Roman chariots and headed for Rapishaw Gap and the impressions made by rubber soled walking boots.

The car park at Housesteads (MR 86/794684) was an ideal starting point and we followed the well-worn path to Rapishaw Gap, and then headed about 20 degrees east of north to cross Jenkins Burn between Greenlee and Broomlee Loughs. The next landmark, heading generally north, was Cragend Farm, along rather vague

123

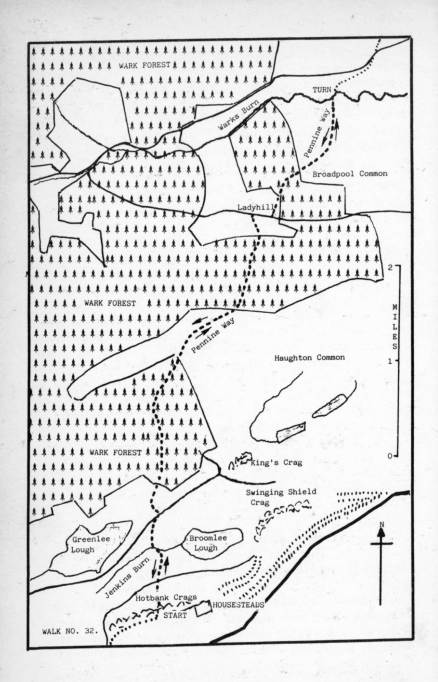

WARK FOREST

Warks Burn

TURN

Pennine Way

Broadpool Common

Ladyhill

WARK FOREST

Pennine Way

Haughton Common

2

M
I
L
E
S

1

0

King's Crag

Swinging Shield
Crag

WARK FOREST

Greenlee
Lough

Broomlee
Lough

N

Jenkins Burn

Hotbank Crags
START

HOUSESTEADS

WALK NO. 32.

124

paths. We crossed the Cragend track and joined the Stonefolds track just as it entered the southern fringe of Warks Forest. The forest path was wide and easy to follow; we ignored side turnings and after about three quarters of a mile, at a fork, we kept to the right. This led us back on to open, damp moorland. Our path was distinct and we re-entered the forest in less than a mile, and headed north to strike a minor road near Ladyhill. Heading east we picked up the north-bound path after about a couple of hundred yards, opposite Lady-hill Farm. A winding path, part through the trees and part over open moor, led us to the deep valley of Warks Burn.

The walk across the flat open moorland was not quite as easy as it looked on the map. Less than half a mile north of the Wall extensive wet patches caused a few diversions and back-tracks, and we found crossing Jenkins Burn made easier by scrambling over a gate that spanned the stream. Then we entered the first real forest of the Pennine Way, conifers planted in rows, with dense beds of needles on the ground. This and the almost total exclusion of daylight prevented the growth of anything on the forest bed. These forests may be more profitable than the old slow-growing deciduous trees that probably grew there in Roman times, but the absence of birds, animals and plants made it a dull, sterile spot.

More wet moors were aheads of us, as we left the wide forest paths, but as we advanced and re-entered the forest we found that our walled path had become a miniature canal. A detour was improvised, we scrambled over walls and fences and regained our path a quarter of a mile further on.

After passing Ladyhill and once again leaving the forest for open moorland, we found it pleasant and dry underfoot. Gorse was in bloom, golden flowers were cresting the dark green foliage and a heady scent filled the air. A few wind-worn trees marked the valley of Warks Burn; we had reached our turning point and had found a lovely picnic spot.

Our plans for this walk had been a little vague regarding the return route. The map showed a possible return via Great Lonbrough, over Haughton Common to Halleypike Lough, but the underfoot conditions near the loughs concerned us. Our pedometer showed that we had walked nine miles and a direct route back would make eighteen. Working on the old adage of a devil you know is better than one you don't, we decided to retrace our steps and possibly save the Halleypike walk for another day.

We followed our outward path as nearly as possible on the return

125

journey. In places we tried to avoid a few of the detours round wet patches, but found others, and finally decided to just plough on.

Dry socks were called for before we got back to Rapishaw Gap, but as our walk was almost finished and we had only a short ride back to camp we didn't worry.

Tomorrow was another day, and we would have an early morning move.

BELLINGHAM TO HARESHAW HEAD (B6320)

(A circular walk of eight miles)

We were up bright and early and moved out of the friendly, well-maintained site, "Seldom Seen" at Haltwhistle at about eight o'clock. Getting back on the B6318 we headed east and picked up a small link road running north that took us to the B6320, which in turn took us straight to Bellingham. The information centre was in the small library in the town centre, and we thought we could collect some information concerning caravan sites. That, strangely, seemed to be outside their province, so we turned to our trusted Camping Club site book and found one listed as Hareshaw Linn at MR 80/944834. This was a site composed largely of static vans, but with friendly residents who showed considerable interest in our venture. We had decided that this must be a short walk so ruling out the link walk that would take us to Warks Burn. A short walk northwards from Bellingham was planned.

Starting from the camp site (MR 80/845835) we headed up the road towards West Woodburn for a few hundred yards until we reached a fairly distinct right hand bend; there we headed almost due north to Blakelaw Farm. A distinct path kept us moving north, with a deep, wooded valley on our left, passing through mainly open pastureland. As we approached Hareshaw House the path swung left a little and reached an open moorland road in about half a mile. We turned there and retraced our steps towards Hareshaw House and searched for a path to take us down the west side of the valley. We headed south on a very vague and doubtful path but met barriers and private signs, and were forced out on to the B6320 road to finish our walk by passing through Bellingham.

This short walk would make a nice Sunday afternoon stroll. The northbound way was a comfortable walk in ideal surroundings, with masses of open views all round. The return was not really satisfactory, but that was possibly our fault because we had not checked it thoroughly beforehand. If we were to repeat this we would follow the same path for both directions. On the trip south there are beautiful views of the north Tyne Valley. An addition

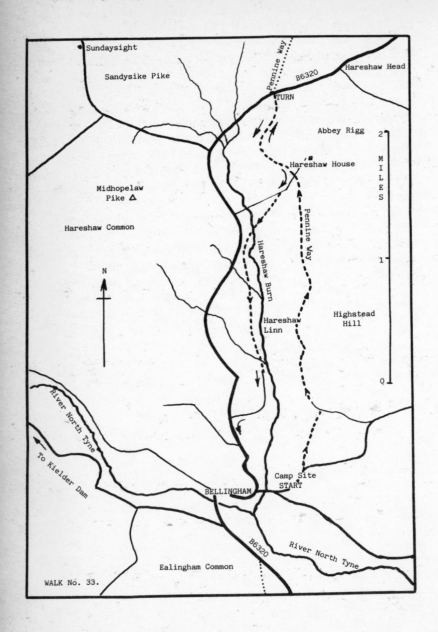

WALK No. 33.

could be made to include the waterfall at Hareshaw Linn. A sandstone outcrop creates this spectacular fall as the Hareshaw Burn plunges about 100 feet to join the North Tyne.

The day was still young when we had finished our walk so we discarded our walking gear and went for a drive to Keilder reservoir. Taking a road south of Bellingham that followed the south bank of the river, we wound our way past little hamlets and isolated cottages for about ten miles. Then a vast expanse of water appeared. Trees in many places came down to the water's edge, but in other places provision had been made for yachtsmen, anglers, campers and caravanners. The surrounding woods were crisscrossed with a multitude of walks and pathways. It was certainly a place worthy of more than a flying visit, but this was not really in our itinerary.

We took the car to the northern end of the reservoir and the village of Keilder, but there was no circular route for cars so we retraced our route to our first point of contact with the reservoir, crossed a bridge to the village of Falstone, and followed a very narrow road back to Bellingham on the north bank of the river.

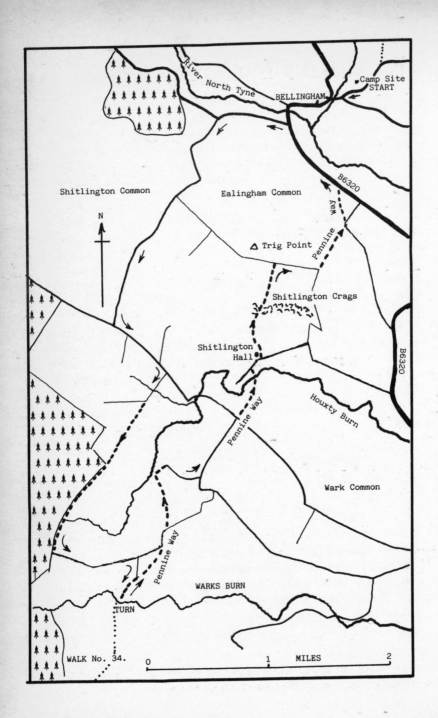

River North Tyne

BELLINGHAM

Camp Site
START

B6320

Shitlington Common

Ealingham Common

N

Pennine Way

△ Trig Point

Shitlington Crags

B6320

Shitlington
Hall

Pennine Way

Houxty Burn

Wark Common

Pennine Way

Pennine Way

WARKS BURN

TURN

WALK No. 34.

0   1   MILES   2

130

WALK 34

WARKS BURN TO BELLINGHAM

(A circular walk of sixteen miles)

Another fine day dawned and another walk was planned. We would fill the gap that had been left by the previous short walk. To make it circular we had planned to use some very minor roads which we presumed would be practically traffic free, especially as we were at the end of Easter week.

Our walk, once again, started at the camp site (MR 80/844834) and back through the centre of Bellingham to join the B6320 south-bound. After crossing the river bridge we took the first road on the right, signposted Keilder, and followed this for a little over a quarter of a mile to a minor road on the left. This minor road, after a short distance, became unfenced and passed West Highridge to a T junction. Our route went left, we ignored the track on our right that led to Hindrigg but chose one about half a mile from the T junction, which led to Watergate. A faint path, running almost southwest took us to the corner of the plantation and we followed the forest fence until we met a minor road close to Warks Burn. Three quarters of a mile to the west we picked up a path to Honeystead and the Pennine Way, and in a few yards our previous picnic spot from walk thirty two.

Gentle easy walking was the only description of the early part of the walk. The surroundings were attractive, but not inspiring. The minor road followed an undulating course with frequent small streams, and the open country was often spongy marsh land. The valley and stream at Warks Burn was still as charming as ever, and we were quite happy to have a second picnic in this spot.

The Pennine Way north from Warks Burn followed the boundary of the National Park and was well defined. It joined the minor road briefly at Ash Farm and left it to take in Linacres, only to twist right to join the minor tarmac road again in a circuitous mile. At the T junction our path went straight ahead to Shitlington Hall, and then north to a single walled track, where we turned right. From there it was downhill to a bend on a minor road and to the B6320, back to Bellingham.

We did not like walking through the regimented plantations of this area, but we found the surrounding open country almost as uninteresting. We were pleased to meet some fellow walkers who were "doing" the Pennine Way north to south, hopefully in one fell swoop. They were accompanied by a small, short-legged dog. He looked dejected, and we would have liked to hear his opinion of the walk, although his master assured us that he always carried the dog when the going was hard.

They tried to cheer us up by telling us how bad it was over the Cheviots, in the distance we could already see them. "Peat bogs stretched for miles," they said, "And the wind howled round the lonely hut that was specially positioned for walkers." They appeared to have spent a stormy night there and their memories were still very vivid. They obviously were not going to believe us if we told them about Kinder Scout, so we kept quiet and gave them the pleasure of finding out. We pitied the poor little dog!

Shitlington Crags made a break in the moor, and we enjoyed the fine view of the North Tyne that it offered, as the river wound its way through more fertile lands. Looking south we could faintly discern the last of the Pennines, and we once again wondered what the Pennine Way was doing in Northumberland. We dropped into rough pasture and agricultural land after leaving Shitlington, and soon picked up the outskirts of Bellingham. We finished our walk, with the traffic, along the B6320.

HARESHAW HEAD (B6320) TO REDESDALE FOREST GATE

(A circular walk of fifteen miles)

This was to be the final walk of the series and it always seemed that we were much harder to please towards the end of a holiday. After a few weeks of suburban existence in our so-called village (which in truth is a dormitory extension of a city) any walk in the country is a wonderful interlude. But after half a dozen walks, with wide open spaces, and none of the hassle of normal living, we automatically become more selective and demanding. Added to this is our mad preference for walking on the tops of hills. We were looking forward to the next holiday when we would experience the Cheviots, but first we had to reach, and pass through, Keilder Forest.

On our previous visit to Hareshaw Head we had cast around for a suitable parking spot. Waste ground on the north side of the road seemed ideal, but there was no easy access, so finally we decided to use a wide verge on the minor road that ran west round Sandysike Rigg.

Leaving the car at MR 80/832878 we followed the B6320 to the Pennine Way crossing, about half a mile ahead, and turned north to Lough Shaw, heading for the high ground. With only a slight deviation to the left we picked up another high point, following a well defined path. The track then led to Lords Shaw Cairn and straight across the Troughend road, where a sign and map confirmed our position. The path then followed close to the fence and fairly close to the monument on Paddon Hill. Due north was Brownrigg Head, but our path made a slight detour to the left and then right, to skirt the damp river head of Dargues Burn. The southwest corner of Redesdale Forest was northwest of us, and we headed for this, and along the forest fence to the gate across the Gibshiel to Blakehopeburnhough road.

As we turned off the tarmac road, past the remnants of old mine workings, our thoughts were on the route ahead, and the occasional glimpses of the Cheviots to the right of our route excited us. The route that we were walking was through comparatively kindly

133

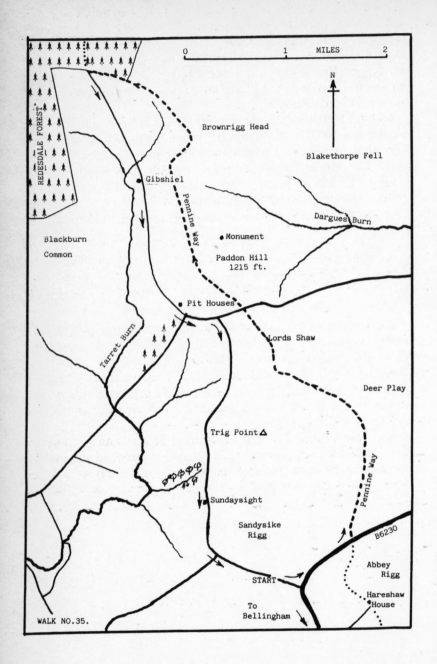

0   1   MILES   2

N

REDESDALE FOREST

Brownrigg Head

Blakethorpe Fell

Gibshiel

Pennine Way

Dargues Burn

Blackburn
Common

● Monument

Paddon Hill
1215 ft.

● Pit Houses

Lords Shaw

Tarret Burn

Deer Play

Trig Point △

Pennine Way

Sundaysight

Sandysike
Rigg

B6230

Abbey
Rigg

START

Hareshaw
House

To
Bellingham

WALK NO.35.

134

terrain. Some patches were damp, but there was little danger of sinking knee-deep in a bog. To avoid the excessively damp places the path searched out the higher ground—Lough Shaw at 1102 feet, Deer Play 1183 feet, Lords Shaw 1167 feet—and then we came to Troughend Road. We picked our way round a large rock on the northern side of the road and followed the well-worn, muddy track adjacent to the rusting wire.

Paddon Hill was our next high point, at 1215 feet, and although we did not go over to inspect the monument, we did pause long enough to identify the Cheviot out of the range of mountains to our right. The Keilder Forest, that was to our left, dark green and foreboding, stretched almost to the skyline, with just a glimpse of reflective water to break the monotony. We went ahead to Brownrigg and then headed for the next man-made forest—Redesdale.

The return journey was all road walking, much of it unfenced. The Gibshiel road took us south to Pit Houses, and the second on our right to Sundaysight. From there the road was walled, but quite devoid of traffic. We kept to the left and rounded Sandysike Rigg to the car.

The open road was, at first, a relief for our legs, but soon became rather boring. After Gibshiel there were attractive views down into the valley with small copses breaking the monotony, and these views improved around the Sundaysight area, but it was with relief that we reached the car. The walk had not been hard but we felt that it was time to go home for a spell and regain our enthusiasm that appeared to be flagging.

Our next series of walks would be from a Camping and Caravanning Club site at Byrness, which is an old favourite of ours, and for the present we could return home knowing that only half a dozen walks remained. Our next walking holiday would complete the Pennine Way.

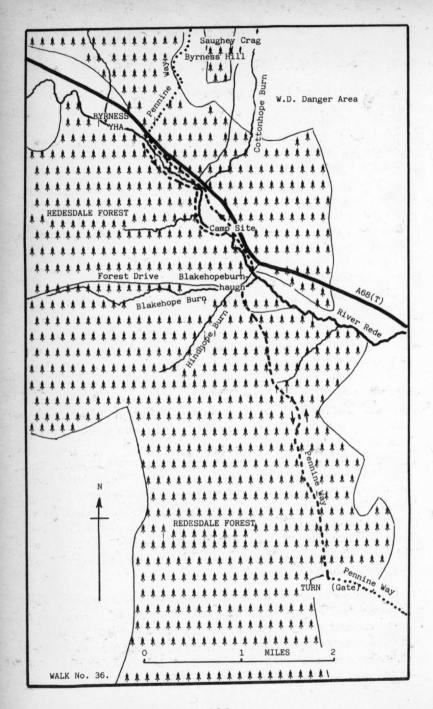

Saughey Crag
Byrness Hill
W.D. Danger Area
Pennine Way
Cottonhope Burn
BYRNESS YHA
REDESDALE FOREST
Camp Site
Forest Drive
Blakehopeburnhaugh
Blakehope Burn
A68(T)
River Rede
Hindhope Burn
Pennine Way
REDESDALE FOREST
N
TURN (Gate)
Pennine Way

0   1   MILES   2

WALK No. 36.

WALK 36
REDESDALE FOREST TO BYRNESS YHA

(An out and home walk of thirteen miles)

We knew that this entire walk was through plantations of conifers, which didn't really enthrall us, but our urgent desire to complete the Pennine Way prompted us and we were driving north again in a little over a month after our previous trip. We did not want to be walking the final stages of our walk when the Spring Bank Holiday crowds were out and about, so our plan was to complete the thirty sixth walk on the Saturday previous to the holiday to make sure that we had completed the Pennine Way by the following Thursday evening.

Our car journey was made on the Friday, heading up the A1 to Scotch Corner, and then up the A68, the Carter Bar road. There was little pleasure driving on the A1 with hundreds of heavy wagons, and the inevitable roadworks. Conditions eased a little on the A68, but traffic was still fairly heavy, and some of the blind crests were quite thrilling. It was a relief to pull into the Camping Club site at Byrness (MR 80/780014). The Byrness site has since closed and it may be necessary to substitute a site in Otterburn as a base for this walk, or find a friendly farmer who would allow a caravan on his land.

Studying our maps there seemed to be some doubt regarding the precise location of the path in the Byrness area. When we had been on the site previously we had frequently seen walkers passing through the camping area and plodding along the road to the YHA. Others had scorned the road and followed a forest path to cross the river upstream. But the map showed a path between the river and the road. We decided to sort this little bit out on the Friday evening by having a short circular walk.

Leaving the camp site we picked a vague path and made our way through small fields, roughly following the right hand river bend upstream, and joined a roadway leading into the village of Byrness. Retracing our steps to the river we crossed over, and followed a wide, shady forest road, with the river away to our left. At the southern end of the caravan site the bridge was crossed back to our van. The

137

following morning we continued our walk by following a track from the bridge on the east bank of the river, which is the official marked Pennine Way route. It led us to a well-wooded picnic area, with all the usual facilities. There we re-crossed the river and entered Redesdale Forest. A wide forest road with wide, sometimes sloping verges was easy to follow and in about three miles the Forest Gate was reached.

This was one of those walks which have no outstanding features but are enjoyable if the season is right. Flowers were beginning to make themselves known, and the air had that Spring freshness. The scent of pines and other conifers were strong, and only bird song broke the silence. The forest road was wide and firm underfoot, the extra width removed the usual oppressiveness of forest walking, but we still prefer the soft turf, or spongy peat, underfoot. In retrospect, there was little that was memorable about that section of the Pennine Way. There were no special, or rare, flowers or birds to record, and we met no one. It was a nice, gentle, breaking-in walk for the first day back. As usual, with out and home walks, we had a picnic at the turning point, sitting with our backs to the fence, the sun in our faces, and our eyes searching for southern landmarks.

The return walk was a steady downhill stroll along the same path, but to ensure that we had covered everyone's interpretation of the Pennine Way we kept to the forest path right through to the camping ground.

On the return journey we noticed the Forest Drive Road, and a couple of cars heading west, apparently having paid the toll. Our map showed this path, in almost unbroken forest, all the way to Keilder, a run of about 12 miles. It was another of those things that made us say "Someday . . .".

BYRNESS YHA TO CHEW GREEN

(A circular walk of fifteen miles)

We looked at the way ahead. Our guides and maps told us that this was the longest stretch without a road crossing. Some books say twenty seven miles of wild, moutainous country, but from experience we have found that most of these figures are based on map measurements, assuming that there are no inclines or diversions, no back-tracking to avoid an impassable peat bog, and no extra half mile to correct an incorrect choice of path. Roads or no roads we had decided that we were splitting this up, and were determined to enjoy our walk through the mountains.

Our part-way target of Chew Green could be achieved as a circular walk only because the army were not using the firing range for exercises. Vast areas of the hills to the east of Redesdale have been commandeered by the army. Tarmac roads have been laid to crisscross the area, but not for the use of the public if the red flags are flying. Notices and flags abound round the perimeter, and before straying into the area it is always wise to make enquiries.

Looking at our map we wondered why we had bothered to make the evening trip to the YHA as the proposed walk actually started there. We started and ended our walk at the camp (MR 80/780014) obivating the need for the car.

We headed up the A68 trunk road towards Byrness, and found the Pennine Way crossing a little before the village turn off. A stiff climb through the trees, up Byrness Hill took us to Saughy Crag. Climbing more gently we passed along the top of Windy Crag to the cairn at Ravens Knowe. This path was easy to follow and practically followed the crest of the hills in a northerly direction. The path dropped down to Coquet Head, and crossed the Scottish border for the first time. Half a mile past the border fence, at a junction of paths, the Pennine Way sign turned us into the valley at Chew Green, and we re-crossed the border fence. A gated, tarmac road was ahead and our furthest point had been reached.

The climb up Byrness Hill called for frequent rests. As with many other map features cartographers seemed to have under-estimated

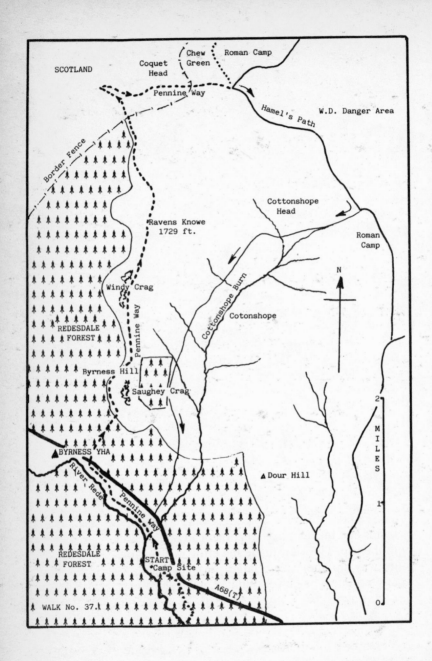

SCOTLAND

Chew Green

Coquet Head

Roman Camp

Pennine Way

Hamel's Path

W.D. Danger Area

Border Fence

Cottonshope Head

Ravens Knowe
1729 ft.

Roman Camp

N

Windy Crag

Cottonshope Burn

Cotonshope

Pennine Way

REDESDALE
FOREST

Byrness Hill

Saughey Crag

2

M
I
L
E
S

BYRNESS YHA

River Rede

Pennine Way

Dour Hill

1

REDESDALE
FOREST

START
Camp Site

A68(T)

WALK No. 37.

0

140

A rather steep climb.

the gradient, or were we getting old? The crags at the top were a
hands and feet climb as we, practically on all fours, panted our way
to the top. The view made the effort worthwhile. The road wound
its way up the valley, large areas of plantation were scattered
around like a patchwork quilt. Catcleugh reservoir glistened in the
sun as miniscule motor cars scuttled past, heading for Carters Bar
and points north.

As we moved on, gaining height, the range of our vision
increased. To our right we could look into Cottonshope Valley,
with the stream gaining strength as it was fed by a mass of small

tributaries. Two lonely farmsteads stood in the midst of this army training area. Cattle and sheep were grazing and we wondered how they fared when the army put up its red flags, and said "Danger—keep out". These hills were so different to our Pennines. Smooth, rounded shapes, gentle, grass-covered slopes, had replaced the harsh, rock-bordered expanses of peat and heathland. We had been warned that this was a hard section—but was it?

Ahead we could see the Cheviot, and the other mountains. In the morning sunshine they looked too benign, but rather far away. We could also see down the Coquet valley with a tarmac road disappearing to the northeast.

We paused at the border fence, a photograph was called for. We stepped into this "foreign" land, and it was no different to our own, so after a few minutes we stepped back again and explored the earthworks of the Roman Camp at Chew Green. After Housesteads and Hadrian's Wall it was a poor experience, but it did provide an excellent spot for a picnic.

For our homeward journey we passed through the gate, ignoring the warning signs, as we had been assured that firing was not taking place, and followed a good tarmac road southeast for about two miles. At a T junction we turned right on a good track, but not tarmac, towards Cottonshope Head, and followed this, running parallel to the main stream, to the plantation ahead. The track improved and we dropped down, through the trees, to hit the A68 almost opposite our campsite.

The walk back was not so scenically exciting. We presumed that our initial stretch of road was the course of the old Roman road, the map called it Hamel's Path, but it linked Chew Green to other Roman camps. The only people we saw were not Romans, or even farmers, but road repair men working on the damaged tarmac. When they heard what we were doing they showed considerable interest, and assured us that there were suitable caravan sites at Coquetdale. These would be useful when we planned our assault on the next section of the Pennine Way through the Cheviot range.

We were somewhat disturbed when we neared the wooded area. Naturally we were approaching the notice board from the rear, but a very tattered red flag was flying from the pole for all to see. Perhaps it had been forgotten, perhaps we had been misinformed, perhaps it was a permanent feature. We shrugged our shoulders and said "So what—we're still safe".

After reaching camp and eating well we made the circuitous trip to Coquetdale, via Otterburn and the B6341. Eventually we reached Alwinton where we saw prominent signs for a caravan site. We continued up the valley to Barrowburn looking for the caravan sites that our helpful roadworkers had promised, but none materialised. Finally, almost in despair, we called at a farm at Barrowburn, but the farmer was not prepared to accept us. The army apparently frowned on the idea, but we were told that there was space further up the valley. We found a spot. The river and narrow road shared the valley bottom, and as the river meandered, and the road ran straight, a wide grass verge of about half a acre was formed.

Across the river notice boards made it clear that the land was reserved for military purposes, but on our side it was obviously the domain of civilians. We parked there. We had our own water and food supply on board and we were fully self-contained. In perfect peace we spent the night!

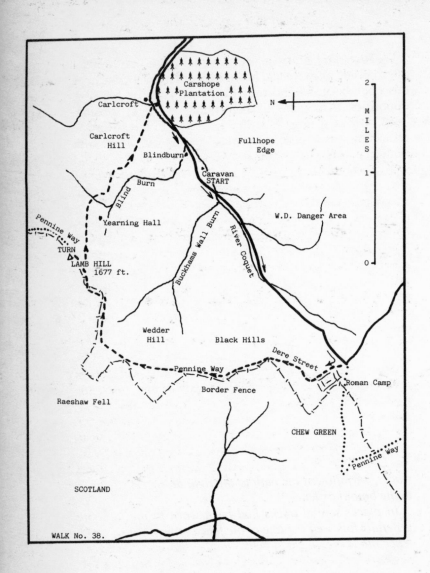

WALK 38
CHEW GREEN TO LAMB HILL
(A circular walk of twelve miles)

We rose early after a peaceful night. In our first twelve hours on our roadside pitch we had heard only one vehicle. The occupants of this open-backed Landrover expressed surprise but no apparent opposition to our unofficial location. In bright sunshine in this deep, sheltered valley, I scrambled down to the stream and had a refreshing wash as skylarks were soaring overhead, with rapidly fluttering wings and continuous melodious song.

To the north of the road were smooth, close-cropped green slopes, but to the south, immediately across the small river, was the almost precipitous slopes of Fulhope Edge and Bell Hill, and the ubiquitous "Danger—Keep Out" notices of the Ministry of Defence. These stated that firing was in progress if the red flag was flying. The proliferation of notices did not bother us but it was probably one of the reaons why so few people ventured up this valley to enjoy the perfect peace of the open country. It seems wrong that anywhere so peaceful should have a warlike connection, or that the lark's song should ever be replaced by the sound of gunfire.

Our walk started from our caravan "somewhere in Coquetdale" and we walked up the deserted tarmac road for about three miles, with the river first on one side and then on the other, and passing three or four farmsteads on the way. As we reached the area of the Roman camp at Chew Green a road turned off to the left and was barred by a closed (not locked) gate. We continued on to the Roman site to pick up the Pennine Way sign, turned right and climbed into the hills. After half a mile, passing through the old Roman earthworks, we followed the path to the right along Dere Street, and then to the boundary fence.

In places several tracks had been worn in the turf, but they all generally followed the line of the fence, moving away only when the fence made inexplicable swings to take in some high spot. After one such diversion the fence made a very sharp turn to the left and then to the right and about a quarter of a mile ahead we saw the Lamb Hill trig point. We decided that we would leave the Pennine Way there and head back for the valley.

145

The road from the van had been an ideal start to our walk, it climbed gently, with only one slight hill. The river chuckled as it splashed over the stones, reminding us that we were climbing. In places large clumps of musk (as kids we called it monkey flower) had become established on the banks or on small islets, and made colourful splashes of yellow and brown against the sparkling water. We passed isolated farmhouses and a farmer's wife told us of the problems of storing winter provisions against the possibility of being completely snowbound for three or four weeks.

On reaching Chew Green and the Roman camps we were once again moved back in time, as we scrambled over mounds and ditches. They really told us nothing, but to the expert they were dwellings and forts, granaries and mess halls. Six pointed stars marked the location of these historic remains, and we used them as markers on our journey. Our map showed Dere Street, and a name on the fence said the same, but all we found as we scrambled over the stile and up the hill was coarse moorland grass, humps, hollows and rabbit holes.

The fence marking the Scottish border (or English border according to one's nationality) was the perfect path guide. In places the map showed footpaths making short cuts, but we tried to keep to the official path. In on particular place, near Raeshaw Fell, the maps said "path undefined", and we quickly found out why. We were back to peaty soil and long brown grass that concealed treacherous pools of dark brown water with boggy surrounds. We avoided what we could, and walked through what we couldn't but not without having boots filled with peat-laden water.

When our target, the trig point at Lamb Hill was reached we were tempted to go a little further but decided against it, and picked up a path that had crossed the border a short distance back and left the Pennine Way.

In the Lamb Hill area the Way runs about northeast and we picked up a path heading east. In a couple of hundred yards, as the path forked, we took the left hand path. This twisted and turned to pass over two minor watercourses and then climbed towards the high spot at Carlcroft Hill. This high point gave us a wonderful outlook over the valley and hillside and we picked out our footpath, running down to Carlcroft Farm on the roadside. A short walk up the road and we were back at the caravan.

Walking in this area was everything we could wish for. Having attained a height of about 1600 feet above sea level, we stayed there, the inclines and declines were unnoticeable. We could see our caravan in the valley, a thousand feet below, and that assured us of an easy downhill finish to our walk. On the gentle slopes of the hills there was very little scrub, and the grass was close-cropped. The native Cheviot sheep, with their white faces and rather aquiline noses, kept these hills in good condition.

The view from Carlcroft Hill was fabulous. We were well up on time, and we sat on the highest point and drank in the beauty. On one side of us Blindburn had cut its water course into the hillside, and tumbled its way down to give that friendly farmer's wife her constant supply of water, and on the other side, Carlcroft Burn was rendering the same service to the homestead at Carlcroft. The valley looked so naturally complete and the road and houses so insignificant. The hills protruded in moulded curves like pie crust on a well filled fruit pie, and there were no sounds except the birds. In this area, largely devoted to pasture, even the intrusive noise of the tractor was missing—and the world slept.

We went down to our man-made road, passing the man-made buildings at Carlcroft and returned to our man-made caravan. Another wonderful day was over as far as activity was concerned, but we still had to consider the rest of the Pennine Way. The next planned walk to Windy Gyle was straight forward, but that would still leave twelve to fourteen miles to do, and this distance would be doubled by returning to our caravan. A suitable splitting point was hard to find. Long, hard climbs on the Scottish side would be called for to achieve only a short walk on the actual Pennine Way. Studying the map, I was pondering this problem when my wife suddenly said "Couldn't we get a taxi to take us to a suitable point, and do it in one go?" I spotted Kelsocleugh, deep in the valley to the north of Windy Gyle, and judged the distance. "Why not?" I said. "It'll be about sixteen miles, but we can do it!"

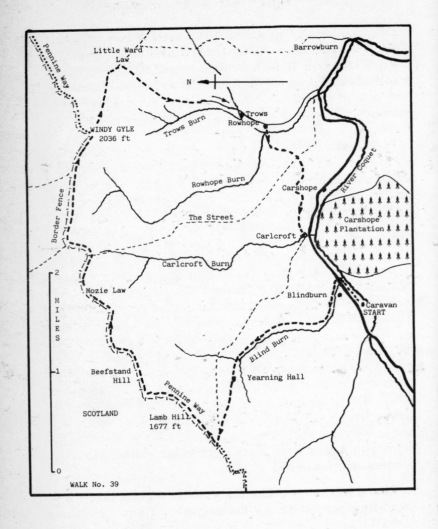

WALK No. 39

148

WALK 39
LAMB HILL TO WINDY GYLE
(A circular walk of eleven miles)

Having made the decision that, by some means or other, we would get transport to the start of our final walk, enabling us to cover Windy Gyle to Kirk Yetholm in one day, we were in high spirits when we prepared for Lamb Hill and our penultimate walk. The end of the Pennine Way was in sight and any doubting moments that we had had during the past eighteen months were forgotten.

The weather was being kind, bright morning sunshine cheered me as I had a cold wash in the clear water of the River Coquet. The dale was maintaining its tranquil air. Road traffic consisted of a military vehicle in each direction daily, and possibly one farmer's vehicle. It was hard to realise that there was a living soul within miles, but we knew that there were four or five active farms on a three mile stretch.

We picked up a footpath that left the road at Blindburn Farm (MR 80/830110) and followed the burn, climbing steadily, in a fairly steep sided valley, and passed the old building which, presumably, was Yearning Hall. After a further half mile we joined the path on which we descended yesterday, and went forward to strike the border fence. We were then back on the Pennine Way, and the fence led us to the trig point at Lamb Hill, 1677 feet above sea level, and then on to Beefstand Hill and Mozie Law. Shortly after that a footpath joined our path from the south, and a gate in a right-angled bend in the fence took the path on to the north. This was The Street. Our path still followed the fence, but a massive cairn also guided us to Windy Gyle. This huge pile of stones and the star marker made this an unmistakable landmark.

Natural features as guides always make walking easier, and the Blind Burn was perfect for the early part of this walk. The map seemed unnecessary, the compass was ignored in the isolation of this valley and surrounding hills. Here and there squelchy ground underfoot forced slight detours, but for over a mile we climbed by the stream, and then the old building "Yearning Hall" appeared. Isolation was complete, natural beauty was everywhere, and we could only assume that it was neighbours and companionship that the original occupier had yearned for.

Having reached the border fence, once again, our navigation was simplified. We climbed to the trig point on Lamb Hill and plotted our course. Easy walking through tussocky grass, we descended slightly only to climb again to Beefstand, at 1842 feet. From there both Windy Gyle and the Cheviot were evident, and our way ahead was clear. All around were rolling mountains, smooth surfaces rounded by nature without the harsh jagged outlines that we had come to expect on the Pennines.

Two special but totally different memories persist from this section of the Pennine Way. Firstly we spotted the flowers of the Cloudberry, a first for us, which only survives near or above 2000 feet. Windy Gyle was listed at 2036. Further back on this Cheviot range we had seen our first and only Orange Hawkweed. It was all alone, we hope no one picked it. The second memory from this high moorland stretch was a sudden glimpse of a valley to the north. It was deep and secluded, and in the flat clearing there was an array of aeroplanes. They looked like last war models, all lined up ready for take-off. Was it a secret army waiting to attack or was it just another bit of this Army training?

Achieving the summit of Windy Gyle was as special landmark, it was 900 feet less than we had managed on Cross Fell, but somehow it rated more highly because we were nearing the end of our walk. As we sat on Russell's Cairn we saw the wide expanse of heather, bilberry and grass, with sheep grazing. The damper patches could be identified by the coarse grass and the swaying white heads of the cotton grass. Looking to the northeast, where the Pennine Way ran, we could see large tracts of peat and we realised that the worst of the Cheviot was still to come.

Leaving Windy Gyle we headed for the high ground to the south-east, Little Ward Law, and then swung to the right, on a slight spur, keeping a small plantation to our left and the Trows Burn to our right. As our path converged on to the stream we picked up a farm track to Trows and Rowhope. There a faint track diverged, climbing a steep bank, and wended its way round Hindside Knowe to Carl-croft, and the Coquetdale road back to our caravan.

The downhill walk to the caravan could really add nothing to the beauty that we already had. The hills and valley were the same and our appreciation of nature and affection for the area was steadfast. These Cheviot walks of eleven or twelve miles, on the pedometer, register as much less, physically. There are no excessive climbs, the terrain is reasonably good, and, for us, the weather had been kind.

Having stuck to our decision to make the balance of the Pennine Way one long walk gave us the added bonus of an extra day, so we agreed to a leisurely move to Town Yetholm on the free day, have a rest, and make our big effort on Thursday. After our evening meal we hitched up and moved the van down the valley to Alwinton, where we had seen the campsite signs. It was a beautiful location, with well kept grounds round a large house. Cabins and lodges were available for hire in the grounds. There was a small shop and the usual caravan park facilities. We did not regret our stay by the river in the midst of nowhere, but we would certainly recommend this Alwinton site to future walkers. Chennel Street passes through Alwinton and is an old drovers' road to Scotland, crossing the Pennine Way at the boundary gate, about one and half miles north-east of Windy Gyle.

The following day, by devious small roads, we found our way to Town Yetholm, pitched on a well kept site, and went looking for a taxi proprietor who would take us to Kelsocleugh in the morning. This was easier said than done but we found the next best thing. The school bus was scheduled to collect a scholar, or scholars, from a farm in the area and we could get transport to a spot near Atton-burn. This added about four miles to our proposed walk, but beggars can't be choosers—so we accepted the offer.

We went to bed early, praying for fine weather and determined to catch that eight o'clock bus.

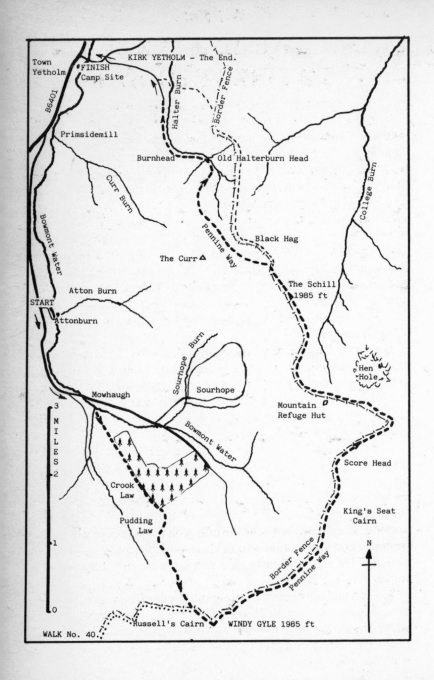

Town
Yetholm

KIRK YETHOLM - The End.

FINISH
Camp Site

Primsidemill

Burnhead   Old Halterburn Head

College Burn

Halter Burn

Border Fence

Curr Burn

Bowmont Water

B6401

Pennine Way

Black Hag

The Curr △

The Schill
1985 ft

Atton Burn

START

Attonburn

Sourhope Burn

Hen
Hole

Mowhaugh   Sourhope

Bowmont Water

Mountain
Refuge Hut

3

M
I
L
E
S

2

Crook
Law

Score Head

King's Seat
Cairn

Pudding
Law

N

1

Border Fence

Pennine Way

0

WALK No. 40.   Russell's Cairn   WINDY GYLE 1985 ft

152

WALK 40
WINDY GYLE
TO KIRK YETHOLM

(A one way walk of twenty one miles)

It was probably the excitement that awakened us early on that Thursday morning. Without getting out of my sleeping bag I eased back the curtain and looked across the river in the direction of Staerough Hill. The trig point on its summit is just under 1100 feet, and it was hidden in mist. My heart sank. Our rule has always been that it was no use going to the top of a hill that was hidden in mist because when you got there you would not be able to see the surrounding country. Nevertheless we rose and dressed, and ate our breakfast, repeatedly glancing at the hill, and willing the mist to rise. Slowly it did improve, the adjacent hill of Shereburgh was clear at 7.45 am, and we walked into the village to catch the school bus. The sun tried to shine, glimmering through the mist like a large white dinner plate.

The garage proprietor, bus driver and campsite owner was one and the same person and we accepted his opinion "You'll have a grand day for it!" We climbed aboard the empty minibus and followed Bowmont Water up the valley. In a little over a mile we left the "B" road and continued up the valley on a narrow, unclassified road.

"How long will it take you?" the driver asked. "All day" was our reply. "We don't rush, we like to look around, sit down, look at flowers or birds, talk about things, and maybe take a photograph."

"We get a lot of the other sort," he retorted. We looked mystified. "Oh", he continued, "they arrive at Yetholm and they've seen nothing. They've rushed over the hills with the sole object of getting from one end to the other as quickly as possible, and it's given them nothing." He was obviously glad that we were not that variety of walker.

The sun had fully emerged as we motored up the valley. The river meandered, with smooth green fields on either side, with sheep and cattle grazing, and not another human being in sight. A track led off to the left and he said "Well this is where I leave you. Have a good walk, see you tonight."

We dismounted and checked our map, we were near Attonburn (MR 74/813227). We hitched our packs and continued up the tarmac lane. After about a mile and a half there were a few houses and farm buildings where the road twisted its way through. There were two small lanes on the right, which we ignored, and then we crossed the river. Almost immediately we re-crossed the river to take a footpath that climbed fairly steeply towards an ancient fort and settlement. The path ran through a plantation for over a mile and passed round Pudding Law, and then on a ridge that ran to the border fence and gate. We then followed a short stretch of our previous walk and followed the fence to Windy Gyle with its large cairn and star marker.

The climb up from Bowmont Water was fairly strenuous, and we hadn't got our "second breath". We had climbed about 1500 feet in two miles, but it had been a climb over lovely, deserted, hillsides, in ideal conditions. Our pedometer showed seven miles since leaving the bus when we had walked for three hours. It was then time to sit, have a drink of tea, and absorb the atmosphere. Not another walker was in sight, a few sheep, a lamb calling for its mother, skylarks, as always, singing on the wing, curlews and lapwings trilling in the distance. Why do we have to have cars and cities? The tea was finished and we knew that ahead of us was a long hard walk.

The path followed closely to the border fence, as we left Windy Gyle, crossing over to the Scottish side for a stretch but returning to the English side at the Chennel Street crossing. The border gate, and Pennine Way board, confirmed our location. Deviations were made from the fence, in some places, due to the squelchy peat and treacherous wet patches. Small cairns helped in some instances, but the fence was the perfect guide over King's Seat and Score Head, and on to the branch path that led to the Cheviot. We ignored the sign to the Cheviot and, from the high spot followed the path (and cairns) leading to the northwest, to find the mountain refuge hut.

Soon after leaving Windy Gyle we had cause to remember the warning that we had been given by walkers in Redesdale. We hit the peat. The general outlook was different to the Pennines, the shape of the mountains, even the type of grass, but the white cotton grass, the pools of water—the colour of tobacco juice—and the black glutinous peat were the same. We floundered through, multitudes of feet had created depressions and these had filled with water. Cairns had been erected to guide and, it seemed some, created by

154

mischievous souls, were meant to deceive. Despite all this we were enjoying ourselves.

From Kings Seat we looked into Scotland, down the valley to Cocklawfoot. We could almost see the spot where we had left the road, it seemed only a stone's throw away, but we had walked almost ten miles. Lunchtime approached and we pushed on to Score Head, found a stretch of hard, firm ground and sat with our backs to the fence to have our picnic.

Hurtling in from Windy Gyle we spotted a figure. As he approached we realised that he was dressed for speed. He carried nothing, wore a pair of shorts and a tee shirt, eyes down, legs pounding, sweat flowing. "Left Byrness this morning," he gasped, "must push on." "Where's your gear?" we asked. "Support team, taking it round by car. Can't stop." He threw the words over his shoulder as he sped away. I don't think he heard our "Goodbye and good luck" but we knew that we had met one of those individuals that the driver had spoken of. We finished our leisurely lunch and contemplated the Cheviot, and agreed that we wouldn't have time to do that—but sometime.

When we reached the refuge hut the terrain had changed. We were on hard, firm ground, across the valley were the crags of Hen Hole, and a steep sided dale stretched away in a northerly direction. We were not seeking refuge but we entered the hut amazed at its location. We wondered who had transported this wheel-less railway cattle truck to this remote spot, and how it had been achieved. We also wondered who had shown so little thought for others that they had left piles of litter. They had stuffed some of it into plastic bags—but who did they imagine would collect them? One has to come to expect such behaviour in cities and areas of dense population, but surely all Pennine Way walkers must have some love and respect for the countryside and natural beauty.

Leaving the refuge hut we were almost immediately confronted by the Schill. Keeping on the English side of the border we climbed this steep slope and followed the fence towards Black Hag. We crossed the border to skirt the summit and then rejoined the fence on the Scottish side and passed along Steer Rig to White Law. About half a mile past the small summit of White Law our path left the border fence and dropped down to Halterburn. We crossed the stream and followed the narrow tarmac road over the hill and then down to the village green at Kirk Yetholm.

The sight of The Schill was frightening, our legs were beginning to feel tired. We promised ourselves that we would have a final cup of tea on the summit and, after frequent rests on the climb, we did. The view was fabulous as we looked down College Burn valley on our right. From the top we felt that it would be all downhill, but it wasn't. We climbed again at White Law, and had the same thoughts as we looked down another valley to Halterburn. We followed the path to cross the stream and join the main road ahead—and then we climbed again. In retrospect it heardly warranted the description climb, it was a gentle slope, but to our weary legs it was a mountain. Over the crest we glimpsed Kirk Yetholm, our spirits rose. We coasted down the slight decline to the village green, the huge notice board, and the end of our adventure.

The experience of having walked the Pennine Way is not easy to put into words. We reached the green, put our arms round each other and said "We've done it". There was no welcoming committee. The only other living creature in sight was a dog, and he was more interested in marking his territory than in us. At the far end of the green there was a pub. If we had walked the entire Pennine Way in one go I suppose we would have been entitled to Wainwright's half pint of beer. But we had done it in our way, we were satisfied, and we enjoyed it. Perhaps, sometime . . .

Happy Ending.

The walk back to the camp was a mixture of physical tiredness and mental elation and then the satisfaction of our bus driver/garage proprietor/site owner saying "Well done".